# Bilbao

Footprint

Andy Symington

# Contents

## Listings

# About the author

**Andy Symington** is from Sydney, Australia. After studying some archaeology and psychology he became embroiled in the world of theatre administration and stage management. Moving into freelance journalism he lived in Edinburgh for two years selling whisky and wine and roaming the highlands before moving to northern Spain. Travel is a passion and he has spent much time in South America and north Africa as well as Europe; he also enjoys prowling around his native land.

# Acknowledgements

Andy would like to thank those people who made it out to Euskadi to help research the eating and drinking sections: Steve, Martin, Theresa, and Jochen; my parents for their support and encouragement, the great team at Footprint, and particularly Riika, a constant companion despite the phone bills and an aficionado of Basque bars in her own right.

Introducing Bilbao

"You appear to have come good," says one Australian to another in a well-known tale. He could have been speaking to Bilbao, the dirty industrial city that has successfully transformed itself into a buzzy cultural capital. And in an amazingly short time, without losing sight of its roots. The Guggenheim Museum is the undoubted flagship of this triumphant progress, a sinuous fantasy of a building that literally takes the breath away. It inspires because of what it is, but also because the city had the vision to put it there. While the museum has led the turnaround, much of what is enjoyable about modern Bilbao was already there. Bustling bar-life, harmonious architecture, a superb eating culture, and a tangible sense of pride in being a working city. The exciting new developments can only add to those qualities. Bilbao is Bilbao because of the Basques. Things are different here; there's a strange language on road signs, weird sports are played to packed houses, it rains an awful lot, and there's a subtle vibrancy that infects even the most mundane of daily tasks.

## Basque separateness

Despite the best efforts of the Basque authorities, terrorism still grabs more column inches in the foreign press than any other issue. It is a serious business but it shouldn't cloud visitors' judgement. ETA is alive, active, and focused, but harming tourists is in complete opposition to its agenda; nearly all their actions are targeted at the Madrid government in some way, or at Basques who are seen as collaborators. A huge majority of Basques deplore terrorism, but this doesn't mean that they don't feel strongly about independence: many do, and they shouldn't be confused with *etarristas*.

## Emerging from the shadows

For forty years under Franco Basqueness was suppressed; the language was banned and the history was falsified. Since his death in 1975 the reawakening of the region has gathered momentum and become an explosion. It's still happening, and it's palpable; as the visitor is discovering the region, the region is rediscovering itself, like a sleeper awakening and stretching limbs.

## 'Basque'-ing in reflected glory

If Bilbao has struggled to re-invent itself, San Sebastián appears to have coasted through on the back of its superb natural setting, a magnet for beachbound visitors since the mid-nineteenth century. Considered one of the peninsula's most beautiful cities, its popularity with backpackers has injected a much-needed dose of youth into the gracefully ageing resort. In contrast to both, Vitoria is a retiring beauty; a quiet achiever combining attractiveness with intelligence: a surprising but suitable capital of the Basque lands. Away from the cities, the things that make a Basque's heart beat loud with the call of ancestors are all still part of rural life: the green hills, the colourful fishing fleets, the slope-roofed stone farmhouses built to last, the *pelota*, the berets. Away from the city's cosmopolitan influences, Basqueness is both evident and accessible.

# At a glance

The Basque semi-autonomous region is divided into three provinces; Bilbao/Bilbo is the capital of Vizcaya/Bizkaia province, San Sebastián/Donostia of Guipúzcoa/Guipuzkoa and Vitoria/Gasteiz of Alava/Araba. The three cities have the feeling of a council about them; distinct personalities united by their different talents and natures in order to make the united whole stronger and wiser. All three are Basque, all three are Spanish. It's a curious duality of which Basque nationalists are wary of, but which is an important factor in the liberal and exciting atmosphere that the visitor can enjoy.

# Bilbao/Bilbo

Bilbao still visibly and proudly wears a blue collar, despite the wealth that industry has brought to large parts of the community, and the city's rapid transformation from polluted urban wasteland to ambitious riverside cultural destination. As folk say in sweeping travelogue generalizations, it's a city of contrasts; from the middle of Bilbao's business district you can frequently see farmhouse-studded green hills to the left and right, while at the estuary mouth wealthy Getxo harbours luxury yachts within a chimney's belch of some seriously heavy waterside industry.

### Casco Viejo (Old Town)

Bilbao's Casco Viejo is a case in point. Its web of attractive streets still evoke a cramped medieval past, but designer clothing stores occupy the ground floors where families perhaps once huddled behind the city walls. Earthy bars serve up thirty-cent glasses of gutsy wine and delicious *tortilla* from a generations-old family recipe while the *pintxos* next door feature imaginative and tasty combinations of goose liver and fresh artichoke. Although most Bilbaínos live and work elsewhere in the city, it's still here that they congregate, to chat, to stroll, to laugh, and to relax.

### El Ensanche

Ensanche, the new town, has an elegant European feel to it. The wealth of the city is evident here, with stately banks and classy shops lining its avenues. Although you can stride across its width in a quarter of an hour, it's divided into *barrios*; the studenty Indautxu, the besuited Abando. At weekends, families roam the shops and the bars and discos crank up for all-night action.

### The Riverbank

The riverbank is the obvious beneficiary of Bilbao's leap into the 21st century: Calatrava's eerily skeletal bridge and Gehry's exuberant Guggenheim bring art and architecture together, making the Nervión river the city's axis once more. Ongoing work aims to further soften the remaining industrial edges.

### Around Bilbao

Bilbao's seaside suburbs, once reached by hours of painstaking river navigation by sweating steersmen, are now a nonchalant 20 minutes away by Metro. Fashionable Getxo has a relaxed beachy atmosphere while, across the estuary, Portugalete is still wondering how Bilbao gets all the credit these days: for hundreds of years it was a far more important port.

## El País Vasco/Euskadi

### San Sebastián/Donostia

Rather like an aristocrat who once worked in a 'suitable' employment while waiting for his inheritance, San Sebastián is past its days as a significant port. Ever since royalty summered here in the 19th century, the city has settled into its role of elegant seaside resort to the manner born. With a superb natural setting, sandy beaches, restaurants, and a regular influx of global stardom during its film festival, it's a relaxed place, recently invigorated by excellent museums and world-class architecture in the Kursaal auditorium.

## Vitoria/Gasteiz

Vitoria is the quiet achiever of the city trio. A peaceful town, it comes as a surprise to many to discover that it's the capital of the Basque region. It is a thoughtful place, the city's young are vocally Basque, and the city feels energized as a result. An attractive old town combines with an Ensanche designed to provide plenty of green spaces for its hard-working inhabitants.

## Inland

Inland, medieval towns such as Oñati, Elorrio and Salvatierra preserve an excellent architectural heritage. Laguardia is one of the most attractive walled towns in northern Spain and an important centre of the Rioja wine region. Gernika has poignant reminders of its martyrdom at Franco's hands. The green hills and rocky peaks of the peninsula are an invitation to the open air. There's excellent walking in Álava, whose rural areas are home to a variety of wild-life. Stray off the main routes and it's easy to find an untouched tract of land to call your own.

## The Basque Coastline

Most of the rural areas are within easy reach of the three cities. Getaria, Mundaka, Pasaia and Hondarribia are picturesque places to visit, while Bermeo, Lekeitio and Ondarroa are still important fishing ports with much to offer in terms of character.

★ **Ten of the best**

**Best**

1 **Bilbao's Casco Viejo** It's tiny but you get lost in it. It's got shops, accommodation, architecture, Basquenes, and some seriously good bars, p33.

2 **Guggenheim Museum** Yes it's good. Even when it's closed it's good. The merits of the art change according to what's on show, but the building is an inspiration, p40.

3 **Laguardia** If you had a perfect mediaeval hilltop village, where would you put it? Slap bang in the middle of top wine country, of course. What more could you want? p114.

4 **Arantzazu Monastery** The Pope wasn't happy, Franco probably wasn't happy. A visionary building for its time, it managed to combine the works of some of the best 20th-century Basque artists. And if you don't like it, you can always take a walk in the superb hills around it, p68.

5 **Calatrava's uplifting bridges** in Bilbao and Ondarroa. He can even make airports beautiful, p39 and p75.

6 **Eating in San Sebastián** Whether it be a gourmet Michelin- starred banquet, a massive feed in a cider house, or a *pintxo* crawl through the old town, p164.

7 **Gernika** Melancholy shrine to Franco's bloodiest slaughter? Not a bit of it. A cheerful and vibrant Basque market town still, strengthened by adversity, p61.

8 **Getaria or Lekeitio or Ondarroa** A Basque fishing town is a very characterful thing, p97, p72 and p75.

9 **Mundaka** A beautiful little place with one of the world's best surf breaks, p70.

10 **Vitoria** A fine city, growing into its role as capital of the Basque country, p98.

# Trip planner

How to spend your time in the Basque lands depends on your perspective. A Bilbaíno was asked his opinion and after a few minutes of deep thought, he came up with the following: "If you have two days, spend a day in San Sebastián and a day in Bilbao. If you have a month, spend a day in San Sebastián and the rest in Bilbao."

Finding the best time to visit Euskadi is partly determined by your priorities. The coast has a very high annual rainfall (mostly drizzle); the driest, hottest time is summer, but it's difficult to find accommodation, and prices rise, especially in the resort towns. The best compromise is to go around May or October, but expect drizzle; the emerald green of the Basque countryside doesn't come for free.

You may want to time your trip around a specific festival. Bilbao's Semana Grande in August, or the Rioja harvest in early October, for example, but be sure to reserve accommodation beforehand. Transport and business hours are often hugely affected by local and national holidays.

The Basque country is very expensive compared with much of Spain, particularly in the eating and drinking department. Accommodation is better value for pairs than solo travellers, but several of the smaller towns lack viable budget options. Fifty euros a day per person would cover a cheap *pensión*, a set meal at lunchtime, some *pintxos* or tapas in the evenings, some drinks and coffees, a couple of sights, and bus or train fares around the region. Eighty per day in a good *pensión* and you won't be counting pennies, with a hundred and fifty per day, you'll be very comfy indeed.

### Short breaks (two-four days)

If you've only got two days, spend them in Bilbao. While it lacks the superb natural setting of San Sebastián, or Vitoria's peaceful picturesqueness, it's a vibrant and honest thinktank, and the premier symbol of the region's rejuvenation and pride in post-Franco Spain. The Guggenheim Museum is a world-class sight on a par with the Golden Gate Bridge or the Sydney Opera House. You might want to head out to Gernika or Mundaka for half a day; both are within easy reach. For seaside appeal stay in San Sebastián, and visit Getaria for a change of scene.

With a little longer at your disposal, you might want to spend two days in Bilbao, a day in San Sebastián, and perhaps stop in Lekeitio or another coastal town in between for fresh grilled fish and beach time. Or you could head down to Vitoria, spend a night in Laguardia, and enjoy a bit of wine tasting.

City lovers might want to simply spend time in the three provincial capitals: an easily achievable aim given the good connections. A day each in San Sebastián and Vitoria will give you a good feel for their charms; Bilbao deserves two days if you've got them.

## Longer breaks (a week or more)

With a week on hand, you could base yourself in Bilbao for the entire time and take day trips. Depending on your timescale, you may have to choose between San Sebastián and Vitoria, if you don't want to rush things. Hit the former if you fancy beaches, sunsets over the water, and style. Choose the latter for peace, Basqueness and class.

If you don't mind moving about, your trip should really include Laguardia, especially if you are a fan of wine and medieval villages; it's a gem. The inland hill towns such as Oñati and Elorrio are proudly Basque, have a noble architectural heritage and are both good spots for striking out with a pair of sturdy boots and a picnic. Basque heritage is divided between these hills, with their distinctive *baserri* farmhouses, and the coast, with its plethora of fishing villages. Historic Lekeitio, Getaria and Hondarribia, with their beautiful harbours, are worth visiting, while Mundaka is a tiny surfing mecca. Any of the beaches would reward for either a night's stopover or a relaxing stay of a few days.

# Contemporary Bilbao

It's official: Europe's oldest people have been reborn, and everywhere the visitor looks there's some celebration or affirmation that it's good to be Basque again. Euskadi is back with a bang, and the old feeling that Bilbao is the centre of the world has rapidly returned.

It's difficult to exaggerate the flowering that has taken place since the return to democracy here. The Basque language, banned during Franco's dictatorship and in danger of a lingering death, has been pounced on by the young and is now spoken widely and ever-increasingly in the streets. There's a touching and understandable feeling that everything Basque is good: to walk into a bookshop to see Tintin and Captain Haddock foiling villains in streams of Euskara gives an idea of how things have changed in quarter of a century.

It seems that everything has been imbued with this 'new Basque' spirit, part of which strives to make the differences between Euskadi and Spain as evident as possible. In this way, the Guggenheim Museum was the perfect project: a daring building that would put Bilbao on the map, attract tourism, add to Basque pride, and blow a raspberry to conservative Madrid. The ruling Basque nationalists gambled that the massive investment would pay off; they were right. Public architecture here has changed for good; the eerily beautiful Kursaal in San Sebastián has been followed by the gleaming Artium in Vitoria. Ghostly Calatrava bridges grace the region's rivers, while even the wineries of baked Rioja have followed suit and commissioned extraordinary lodges to receive grapes and visitors in.

Side by side with architectural inventiveness has marched the revival in Basque art. You can't go half an hour without coming across the works of the two pre-eminent Basque sculptors: the fluid emotion of Oteiza or the late Chillida's twisting explorations of space. These two very different personalities (see box, p83) are rightly considered as ambassadors that carry Basque culture far

*The unmistakeable silhouette of Bilbao's Guggenheim stands out against a brooding Basque sky. The museum's daring lines are symbolic of the region's explosive regeneration.*

outside Euskadi. The appreciation of Basque artists, and the promotion of young writers, painters and actors is all part of the wave: readings of new Euskara poetry are frequent and popular (many listeners are still learning the language).

If one thing apart from the Guggenheim is guaranteed to delight first-time visitors, it's the food, or more accurately food culture. From about half-seven in the evening until midnight or so, everyone lives in the street, walking, talking, drinking and eating *pintxos*. Walk into a bar in any Basque city or village and the counter will be laden with snacks, from a traditional slice of tortilla to a sleek designer creation. Basque restaurants are, and always have been, superb, but this way of snacking has an irresistible appeal. "Why don't we do this back home?" is everyone's thought.

While traditional Basque activities such as *pelota*, stone-lifting and log-chopping are far from being anachronisms – popular with young and old – the two things that make Euskadi tick are politics and football, which are often indistinguishable. Athletic Bilbao and to a lesser extent Real Sociedad and Alavés regularly carry the Basque flag into battle against the Spanish enemy. Athletico only employ Basque players, playing every game with a nation behind them. During the Franco years supporting Los Leones was one of the few ways to show Basqueness, and they remain a massive symbol.

Politically the three Basque provinces are "semi-autonomous"; their parliament has the right to generate their own taxes, among other things. Although most Basques see this constitutional arrangement as the best way to pursue either nationalist or federalist goals, the minority that supports a more radical route to freedom is significant. ETA, responsible for over 800 deaths in the last forty years, are alive and currently still locked in a spiral of recriminations with the rightist Spanish government of José María Aznar. For every ETA atrocity, the torture of a prisoner or an "accident" levels the score and prolongs the cycle. In August 2002, after a purpose-built bill was resoundingly passed in parliament, the courts banned Batasuna, the political party frequently seen as being linked to ETA; it remains to be seen how this provocative and undemocratic gesture will aid the peace process. Frequently overlooked are the large Spanish population of the Basque provinces, who are caught in a situation that is not of their making and from which they have precious little to gain.

Most travellers arrive in Bilbao by plane. The cheapest direct flights from the UK tend to be with the budget operators, although scheduled flights with international airlines often end up cheaper if you are flying at a weekend with less than a month's notice. The only international airport in Basque Spain is in Sondika, Bilbao. It's a beautiful brand new building designed by Santiago Calatrava, seemingly in homage to the whale, located 10 kilometres north east of the centre. Bilbao and the Basque Country can also be reached by bus and train from the UK. They are unlikely to save you time or money, but it can be more pleasurable, and you do have the added advantage of being able to stop along the way.

# Getting there

## Air

*From UK, Europe and Spain*  Flights with **Go** (bought out by **Easyjet** in 2002, standard routes remain operational) can be as low as £30 return from London Stansted, but are more usually £60-120. It's easier to get hold of a cheaper fare if you fly off-season or midweek, and if you book well in advance. **Ryanair** has a budget route from London Stansted to Biarritz, France. It's easier to get cheap seats on this flight, although the taxes are fairly high. Biarritz is half an hour on the train to the border, from where it's another half-hour to San Sebastián. The other advantage of Ryanair is that one-way flights are feasible, while on Go a return effectively has to be purchased. Bilbao is also served from London by **Iberia** and **British Airways** . APEX fares tend to be about £110-140 return and can be more economical if connecting from another British city. These scheduled airlines offer greater flexibility. Bilbao is directly connected with several other European cities, including Frankfurt, Zürich, Brussels, Paris and Milan. The airlines operating these routes often have reasonable prices for connections from London. Try **Lufthansa** or **Air France**.

Connecting via other Spanish cities is another option. **Iberia** connects Bilbao with most major Spanish cities, while **Spanair** and **Air Europa** also operate some flights. Flights are fairly expensive, with a typical Madrid-Bilbao return being about €150. Iberia's website, however, has some excellent last-minute specials that can bring the price down as low as €50. These are released on Thursdays and are accessed through the *entrando en pista* section of their website. If flying into Madrid from outside Spain, onward flights are often added at little extra cost. There are also flights from Madrid to San Sebastián and Vitoria.

**Airlines and agents websites**

www.aa.com **T** 1800 433 7300
www.airfrance.com **T** 0845 0845 111
www.britishairways.com **T** 0845 77 333 77
www.delta.com **T** 1800 241 4141
www.dialaflight.com **T** 0870 333 4488
www.ebookers.com **T** 0870 050 0808
www.easyjet.com **T** 0870 6 000 000
www.expedia.com **T** 0870 010 7000
www.go-fly.co.uk **T** 0870 607 6543
www.iberia.es **T** 0845 601 2854
www.lufthansa.com **T** 0845 7737 747
www.ryanair.com **T** 0871 246 0000
www.usairways.com **T** 1800 622 1015

*From North America* There are no direct flights to Bilbao from North America, so it´s best to connect in Madrid, Barcelona, London or Paris. From the east coast flights can rise to about US$1500 in summer, but in winter, or with advance purchase, a return to Madrid can be as low as $400. Prices from the west coast are usually only US$100 or so more. **Iberia** fly direct to Madrid from many east coast cities, while other airlines offering reasonable fares are **American Airlines**, **Delta** and **US Airways**.

*Airport Information* A taxi from the airport to/from Bilbao costs about €15-20. An efficient and cheap bus service runs to/from Plaza Moyúa in central Bilbao and takes 20-30 minutes. It leaves from the airport terminal, Monday to Friday, every 30 minutes at 15 and 45 minutes past the hour, Saturday hourly at 30 minutes past. From Plaza Moyúa Monday to Friday every 30 minutes on the half-hour, Saturday hourly on the hour. One-way €0.95.

## Road

*Bus*  **Eurolines** runs a bus that leaves London Victoria at 0800 on Monday and Saturday, and arrives in Bilbao at 0430 the next morning. The return leaves Bilbao at 0030 on Thursday and Saturday night, getting to London at 1945 the next evening. There's an extra bus in summer. A return costs about £100; concessions available. Bookings on 01582 404 511 or www.gobycoach.com

Bilbao, San Sebastián and Vitoria are connected with most major Spanish cities by bus. Long-haul services are efficient, fast and cheap. Check the journey time when booking, as there's the odd "all stations to" service. A bus from Madrid to Bilbao costs about €21, making it cheaper and faster than the train.

## Sea

**P&O** runs a ferry service from Portsmouth, but in reality it's more of a cruise than a connection. The ship, *Pride of Bilbao*, is the largest ferry operating out of the UK and has several restaurants, a cinema, pool, sauna and casino. None of which comes cheap – at least £400-500 return for two people with a car. It's a two-night trip, cabin accommodation is mandatory. Boats leave Portsmouth at 2000 on Tuesdays and Saturdays, except during winter, when there are few crossings. The return ferry leaves Bilbao on Thursdays and Mondays at 1230. Book online at www.poportsmouth.com (it's frequently off sick) or on T 0870 242 4999. The ferry port is at Santurtzi, 13 kilometres from the city centre.

A cheaper and faster option is the **Brittany Ferries** service from Plymouth to Santander, 100 kilometres west of Bilbao. These leave the UK on Monday and Thursday mornings, taking just under 24 hours. Return ferries leave Santander on Tuesday and Thursday. Book online at www.brittanyferries.co.uk or by phone on 08705 561 600. Prices are variable but usually around £70-90 each way in a reclining seat. A car adds about £140 each way, and cabins start from about £80 a twin. The service doesn't run in winter. Check www.ferrysavers.com (0870 442 4223) for cheaper offers.

### Train

Using **Eurostar** (www.eurostar.com, T 0870 160 6600), changing stations in Paris and boarding a **TGV** to Hendaye can have you in San Sebastián 10-11 hours after leaving Waterloo if the connections are kind. Once across the Channel, trains are reasonably priced, but factor in £100-200 return on Eurostar and things don't look so rosy, unless you can take advantage of a special offer. The train/ferry combination will virtually halve the cost and double the time.

Bilbao is linked by train with the rest of Spain by **RENFE**. A train from Madrid to Bilbao costs about €37 but is slower than the bus. Book online at http://horarios.renfe.es

## Getting around

Bilbao is a very walkable city, as are San Sebastián and Vitoria. For further-flung parts of Bilbao, such as the beach or the bus station, or to save tired legs, the Metro is an excellent service. New, fast and efficient, it's a claustrophobe's dream and runs until about midnight Sunday to Thursday, until about 0200 on Friday nights, and all night Saturdays. A single fare costs €1, a day pass is €3. There's one main line running through the city and out to the beach suburbs, the recently opened second line will eventually reach the coast too.

Although there's a reasonable network of local bus services in Bilbao, they are only generally useful for a handful of destinations; these are indicated in the text.

Bilbao's long-absent trams are shortly to make a welcome come-back and will hopefully ease traffic congestion in the city centre.

### Bus

*Bilbao/Bilbo*  The majority, but by no means all, of Bilbao's interurban buses leave from the Termibus station near the football stadium (Metro: San Mamés). All long-haul destinations, including San Sebastián and Vitoria, are served from here, but several Basque towns are served from the stops next to Abando station on Calle Hurtado Amezaga or by the tourist office on the Arenal. Buses to Vitoria leave about every 30 minutes with **Autobuses La Union**, 55 minutes, €4.50, and to San Sebastián, every 30 minutes weekdays, every hour at weekends, operated by **PESA** and **ALSA**, 1 hour 20 minutes, €5.93

*The Basque Country*  Most interurban buses from San Sebastián leave from the main bus station on Plaza Pio XII. There are regular services to Basque destinations, Madrid (**Continental**), and most major Spanish cities. The company offices are on Paseo Vizcaya and Avenida Sancho el Sabio on either side of the bus bays.

San Sebastián to Bilbao; every 30 minutes weekdays, every hour at weekends, operated by **PESA** and **ALSA**, 1 hour 20 minutes, €5.93; San Sebastián to Vitoria; seven buses daily, **ALSA**, 1 hour 45 minutes, €6.55. Shorter-haul buses to Guipúzcoan destinations leave frequently from the central Plaza Guipúzcoa. Destinations include Zumaia, Zarautz, Azkoitia, Tolosa, Oiartzun, Hernani, Astigarraga.

Vitoria's bus station is just east of town on Calle Los Herrán. To Madrid; nine daily departures, seven to Logroño, and several to other Spanish centres. Vitoria to Bilbao; from the bus station about every 30 minutes with **Autobuses La Union**, 55 minutes, €4.50. Vitoria to San Sebastián; seven buses a day with **ALSA**, 1 hour 45 minutes, €6.55.

## Car

*Bilbao/Bilbo*  Driving in Bilbao can be frustrating, with a complex one-way system, heavy traffic and ambiguous signs. The most convenient places to park are the numerous, but expensive, underground stations, €10-12 a day. Metered areas are cheaper, but you can't load them up for the whole day. Metered zones are indicated by a solid blue line, a dotted blue line marks a zone where there's a time-of-day factor, which will be signposted. If there's no line, it's a free zone, but they're few and far between in the centre. There are free carparks near the Begoña basilica and next to Sarriko metro station, beyond Deusto, but they're not especially secure. For paid long-stay parking, follow the signs off Plaza del Ayuntamiento.

*The Basque Country*  Driving around San Sebastián and Vitoria, and exploring the Basque region, is relatively easy by car. Apart from the usual precautions, the main nuisance are the tolls on the *autopistas*, which are extortionate. Avoiding these roads often means watching the back of a truck for long stretches on the free but slow *rutas nacionales*. Petrol costs from €0.80–€0.95 per litre.

## Cycling
Bilbao isn't especially cycle-friendly, but it's a good option for exploring the surrounding countryside. San Sebastián and in particular Vitoria are good two-wheel cities, with more planned cycleways and green spots than in busier Bilbao. Getxo is a good area to explore by bicycle, as indeed is most of the Basque coast; the trip between Bilbao and San Sebastián is a particularly rewarding ride, with only a handful of steep sections.

## Taxi
Taxis are prevalent, both on the street and at cab ranks. If the green light on top is on, they're free. Drivers will only enter the narrow streets of the old towns if summoned. Sample fares: Casco Viejo to Guggenheim, about €5-6; San Sebastián's Parte Vieja to Monte Igueldo, about €7 to the top; Vitoria's train station to the basilica at Armentia, €5; Bilbao centre to Getxo, €14.

## Train
Bilbao/Bilbo  Bilbao has three train stations. The main one, Abando, is the terminal of **RENFE**, the national Spanish railway. It's far from a busy network, and the bus usually beats it over a given distance but it's the principal mainline service. Abando is also the main terminus for Euskotren, a handy short-haul train network which connects

Bilbao and San Sebastián with many of the smaller Basque towns as well as their own outlying suburbs. The other Bilbao base for these trains is Atxuri, just east of the Casco Viejo. Trains to San Sebastián leave every hour on the hour (2 hours 39 minutes), €5.50, via Zarautz, Zumaia, Eibar, Durango. An attractive but run-down station for lines running eastwards as far as San Sebastián, and particularly useful for reaching Euskadi's coast towns. Gernika is serviced every hour (18 minutes past, 53 minutes) and on to Mundaka and Bermeo. Finally private FEVE trains connect Bilbao along the coast to Santander and beyond. They are slow but scenic and leave from the Estación de Santander just next to Bilbao's main Abando railway station.

*The Basque Country* San Sebastián's main terminus here is the Estación del Norte just across the river from the new town area. The Euskotren hub is Amara, on Plaza Easo in the south part of the new town. Trains to Bilbao leave from Amaro station every hour, 2 hours 39 minutes, €5.50. To Vitoria, 11 trains a day leave from Estación del Norte, 1hour 30 minutes to 2 hours, €12 (or less, depending on service).

Vitoria's **RENFE** station, south of the centre at the end of Calle Eduardo Dato, has better connections with Spain than Bilbao. To San Sebastián, 11 trains a day leave from the RENFE station.

## Walking
Bilbao is no London or Madrid; it's a relatively small place, and easily walkable. The Guggenheim Museum is an easy 15 minutes along the river promenade from the old town. Much of the charm of the Basque cities is absorbed simply by strolling around. The *paseo*, or *txikiteo*, is a particularly enjoyable time to be afoot; from about 1930-2030, everyone takes to the streets, with family or friends, and simply walks, with not a hint of hurry or destination. The old town is a focus for this, as is Bilbao's riverbank, San Sebastián's beachfront, and Vitoria's Calle Dato.

**Travel extras**

### Police distinctions
There are three main types of police operating in Euskadi.
**Guardia Civil**: Hated by the Basques for their frequent
repressionist tactics and torture of prisoners, this national force
dressed in green are responsible for the roads, borders, and law
enforcement away from towns. Not a bunch to get on the wrong
side of but civil to tourists. **Policia Nacional**: Responsible for most
urban crimefighting, these brown-shirted folk are the ones to go
to if you need to report anything stolen, etc. **Ertzaintza**: The most
dashing force in the region, with cocky red berets, they are a
Basque force who deal with day-to-day beat policing.

### Safety
The Basque country is an extremely safe place to travel. As
everywhere, you should be cautious with your belongings but there's
no tourist-crime scene as there is in Barcelona or Madrid. Danger from
terrorist or police violence is minimal, but steer clear of controversial
demonstrations or events. There are dodgy areas in Bilbao; the very
sleazy red-light area around Calle San Francisco across the river from
the old town is dangerous night and day, and you should avoid the
tunnel under the Puente de Arriaga if you're squeamish about
needles. San Sebastián and Vitoria are extremely safe unless you get
on the wrong end of an argument about football.

### Tipping
Tipping in Spain is far from compulsory, but much practised. Ten per
cent is considered fairly generous in a restaurant, but not excessive.
It's rare for a service charge to be added to a bill. Waiters do not
normally expect tips for lunchtime set meals or tapas. In bars and
cafés people will often leave small change, especially for table service

# Tours

## Adventure tourism

There are several adventure-tourism organizations, who organize a range of activities across the provinces. The best are: **Euskal Abentura**, C Salvador 16, Bilbao, T 943-214870, www.ehabentura.net  An adventure company organizing a massive range of outdoor activities throughout Euskadi. **Getxo Abentura**, an initiative of the Getxo tourist office, will organize just about any outdoor activity in the Getxo area, from caving to canoeing.  **Ludoland**, C Herrería 25, Vitoria, T 90-2293000, www.ludoland.net  Offers all manner of outdoor pursuits, including skiing, rafting, canyoning, hiking. **Soka Viajes**, Gerlasio Aramburu 6, Pasaia, T 943-527142. **Troka Abentura**, C Zabalbide 26, Bilbao, T 944-334728, www.troka.com  Bungee-jumping, abseiling, caving, mountain-biking, hot-air balloon rides. Last, but far from least, **Tura**, T 945-312535, based out of the tourist office in Salvatierra, organizes a range of activities throughout Alava province.

## On and in the water

There are a number of enjoyable ways to cruise the Nervión, explore the Urdaibai estuary, or generally get wet:

**Barco Pil-Pil**, Bilbao, T 944-465065. Trips April-October Saturday/Sunday, July/August Tuesday-Sunday, €9.30, one-hour trip and drink. Dinner and dance cruises, four hours, all year Friday/Saturday, €49.50, book in advance as the meal is pre-prepared by caterers. Leaves from a jetty not far from the Guggenheim Museum. The **Euskal Herria** boat does the trip from Getxo-Portugalete via Santurtzi, leaving Getxo hourly on the half-hour and Portugalete hourly on the hour. The jaunt across the rivermouth takes 30 minutes.

In Getxo, **Maremoto Renting**, Puerto Deportivo de Getxo, T 65-0439211, rents out jet-skis, sailboards and runs trips. **Náutica Getxo**, Puerto Deportivo de Getxo, T 60-9985977, on the jetty at the end of Ereaga beach, yachts with or without a skipper.

**Barco de Ocio**, San Sebastián, runs trips around the bay, half-hour duration, Saturday and Sunday hourly departures, €5.50, leaves from half way along aquarium wharf. **K-Sub**, C Trinidad 2, Zarautz, T/F 943-132472, runs PADI scuba courses.

**Aixerreku Urdaibai Nature Guides**, Ap de Correos 234, T 94-6870244, www.euskalnet.net/aixerreku Eco-cultural tours of the Urdaibai reserve, and birdwatching excursions.

### Cycling and walking tours
**Amaiur**, C General Concha 8, Bilbao, T 944-440552, www.castilloamaiur.com **Bisertur**, C Gardoki 7, Bilbao, T 944-153606, www.bisertur.com Offers half-day and day tours of Bilbao and longer regional tours, mainly in Spanish. **Euskaltrip**, Paseo Colon 17, San Sebastián, T 943-290185, www.euskaltrip.com Transfers, reservations, and cultural tours of San Sebastián and Euskadi. **Stop Bilbao**, Gran Vía 80, Bilbao, T 944-424689, www.stopbilbao.com Guided tours, accommodation and restaurants. **Tenedor**, T/F 34-943313929, tenedor@euskalnet.net English-speaking tours from a Basque-based company.
**The Walking Connection**, 4722 W. Continental Drive, Glendale, AZ 85308, T1 (602) 978-1887, www.walkingconnection.com

### Sightseeing tours
**Bilbao Paso a Paso**, T 944-730078, runs knowledgeable tours of Bilbao and the whole of Euskadi. There's a **San Sebastián sight-seeing bus** that runs Monday, Wednesday, Thursday, three times a morning, and Friday-Sunday three times a morning, twice in the afternoon. Ticket (€9) valid for 24 hours, hop-on, hop-off, at 17 or 25 stops. In San Sebastián a small tourist 'train' leaves every hour from Teatro Victoria Eugenia, T 943-288027. Guided tours of **Guernika** leave at 1100 from the tourist office, T 94-6255892.

### Special-interest tours

To enter the world of the San Sebastián culinary societies, try an **Epiculinary** tour; all-inclusive events include several gourmet meals and cooking lessons from society members. Pathfinders, Stita House, 1 Bath Street, Cheltenham, Gloucestershire GL50 1YE, T 44 (1242) 515712, www.pathfinders.co.uk Runs food and wine tours in the Basque country and Rioja. Totally Spain, Calle San Prudencio 29, Edificio Ópera, Piso 3º, Oficina 62-B, 01005 Vitoria-Gasteiz, www.totallyspain.com T 34-945141538, T 0709-229-6272 (UK). Organizes tours, accommodation and transport.

*There are excellent walking opportunities in the peaceful painted forest of Oma, near Gernika.*

# Tourist information

Bilbao's excellent tourist office is at Paseo del Arenal 1,
T 944-795760, bit@ayto.bilbao.net  *Open Mon-Fri 0900-1400 and
1600-1930; Sat 0900-1400; Sun 1000-1400*. There's also a small
office by the Guggenheim Museum at Abandoibarra Etorbidea 2,
*Tue to Sat 1100-1400 and 1600-1800; Sat 1100-1400 and 1700-1900;
Sun 1100-1400*. The city's website (www.bilbao.net)
is also a good source of information.

All tourist offices in Euskadi have an excellent range of material
and also have comprehensive maps on sale for €2-3. San
Sebastián's city tourist office: Calle Reina Regente 3, T 943-481166,
F 943-481172, www.sansebastianturismo.com  *Open Mon-Sat
0900-1400, 1530-1900; Sun 1000-1400*. In Vitoria: head for either the
efficient city tourist office conveniently set on Calle
Eduardo Dato 11, *open Mon-Sat 1000-1900, Sun 1100-1400*,
or the Basque government office at the southwestern corner of
Parque de La Florida, *open Mon to Sun 0900-1300, 1500-1900*.

## Casco Viejo  33

Bilbao's old quarter is the most charming part of town, a lively jumble of pedestrian streets that has always been the city's social focus.

## Riverbank  37

The Nervión riverbank has been and continues to be the focus of most of Bilbao's beautification schemes. Tourists flock to Gehry's Guggenheim, the most emblematic symbol of Bilbao's rejuvenation.

## El Ensanche  45

The elegant new town, where sleek tower blocks flank designer shops and hip bars along leafy avenues.

## Deusto  50

The university district. Historically a separate parish, it still feels like a town of its own with an alternative vibe.

## Around Bilbao  51

At the mouth of the estuary of the Nervión, Bilbao's beach suburbs make a great day trip from Bilbao, as it's all easily connected by Metro with Bilbao.

# ★ Casco Viejo

*Tucked into a bend in the river, Bibao's old town has something of the medina about it; on your first few forays you surely won't end up where you might have thought you were going. The parallel **Siete Calles** (Seven Streets) are the oldest part of town, and even locals struggle to sort out which bar is on which street. While there aren't a huge number of sights per se, there are dozens of quirky shops and some very attractive architecture; leisurely wandering is in order. The true soul of the Casco emerges from early evening on, however, when Bilbaínos descend on the Casco like bees returning to the hive, strolling the streets, listening to buskers, debating the quality of the pintxos in the myriad bars, and sipping wine in the setting sun.*

▸▸ *See Sleeping p123, Eating and drinking p150, Bars and clubs p177 Arts and entertainment p188*

## The Siete Calles
*Metro: Casco Viejo. Map 1, E3, p247*

In 1300 the lord of the province of Vizcaya, Don Diego López de Haro V, saw the potential of the fishing village of Bilbao and granted it permission to become a town and by the end of the 14th century the town had three parallel streets: Somera, Artekale and Tendería (street of shopkeepers). These were soon added to Belostikale and Carnicería Vieja, with Barrenkale and Barrenkale Barrena coming to the party. These make up the Siete Calles, the seven original streets of the city. It was a time of strife, and the fledgling town was walled, but, at the end of the 15th century, the original fortifications came down and the city began to grow.

**!** Bilbao's city's coat of arms features two wolves; the family symbol of Don Diego whose family name López derives from the Latin word *lupus*, wolf...

The Siete Calles today bristle with bars and shops. Somera is a particularly interesting street; there's an alternative feel about it, and the watering holes are proudly Basque.

## Catedral de Santiago
Plaza Santiago.  *Metro: Casco Viejo.  Map 1, E3, p247*

The slender spire of this graceful Gothic cathedral rises from the very centre of the tightly packed Casco Viejo. Mostly built in the late 14th century on the site of a previous church, it was devastated by fire in the 1500s and lost much of its original form. Two of its best features are later additions: an arched southern porch, and a small but harmonious cloister (if it´s locked, the attendants will open it). Promoted to cathedral in 1950, the building has benefitted from recent restoration.

## Plaza Nueva
*Metro: Casco Viejo.  Map 1, C2, p247*

One of a series of similar cloister-like squares in Euskadi, the 'new' square was finished in 1849. Described by Unamuno as "my cold and uniform Plaza Nueva", it will particularly appeal to lovers of geometry and symmetry with its courtly, neo-classical arches. These arches conceal an excellent selection of restaurants and bars, with some of the best *pintxos* in town on offer. In good weather, most have seating outside in the square. If the centre seems a little empty, it is; in the past it has housed a statue, a bandstand, and, most recently, a fountain. The area, cleared for the construction of the underground car park, comes to life on Sundays, when there's a flea market. At Hallowe'en, the square is a riot of colour, as thousands of floral wreaths for All Saints' Day are sold.

## San Nicolás de Bari

Arenal s/n. *Metro: Casco Viejo.* Map 1, C2, p247

The Baroque façade of this 18th-century church dominates the Parque del Arenal and is attractive when sunlit. When Bilbao was a village, this was the fishermen's quarter, and there was a tiny chapel here dedicated to Nicolás, patron saint of sailors. As Bilbao grew, it was decided to replace it with a larger church; the half-finished result suffered through two centuries of *mañanas* before being demolished and replaced with the current church. Inside, it's spacious but fairly uninteresting.

● *Behind the church, on grimy Calle Esperanza, is a frontón where there are frequent games of pelota, both organized and informal.*

## Museo Arqueológico, Etnológico y Histórico Vasco

Plaza Miguel de Unamuno 4, **T** 944-155423. *Tue-Sat 1100-1700, Sun 1100-1400. €3 (free on Thu). Metro: Casco Viejo.* Map 1, D4, p247

Attractively set around an old Jesuit college, this museum houses an interesting if higgledy-piggledy series of Basque artefacts and exhibits covering thousands of years. There's a fascinating room-sized relief model of Vizcaya on the top floor, a piece of one of the Gernika oak trees, and some good displays on Basque fishing, as well as a decent but poorly presented series of prehistoric finds. Descriptions are currently in Euskara and Spanish only, although English panels are being mooted. The museum's centrepiece is the boarlike *Mikeldi*, of uncertain prehistoric origin.

The slightly shabby plaza, named for the great Bilbao poet and philosopher Miguel de Unamuno, gets very rowdy indeed on Saturday nights, when it's the gathering place for crowds of under-age drinkers. Unamuno himself was born in a house on nearby Calle Ronda: a defaced plaque is the only evidence.

## Basilica de Begoña

*Begoña s/n. Buses 3 and 30 from Plaza Circular, Bus 41 from Gran Vía. Metro: Casco Viejo (take the Begoña exit) or the lift from Calle Esperanza (€0.25), at street level, bear right, then turn right up Calle Virgen de Begoña. Map 1, A6, p247*

Atop a steep hill above the Casco Viejo is Bilbao's most important church, home of Vizcaya's patron the Virgin of Begoña. It's built in Gothic style on the site of a chapel where the Virgin is said to have appeared in former times. The 13th-century idol occupies a niche in the central *retablo*. The cloister is a later addition, as is the flamboyant tower, which gives a slightly unbalanced feel to the building. Within the basilica is the painting *La Coronación Canónica de la Virgen de Begoña*, an impressive work by the 19th-century Basque painter known as *Echena*, and paintings by Giordano.

From the Casco Viejo, take the lift from Calle Esperanza or leave the Metro station by the Mallona exit. From there, walk up the hill to the basilica. The park on your left is **Etxebarria**, formerly a factory complex. One of the chimneys has been left for good measure. From here are excellent views of the town, but you can ascend further, behind the basilica, for even better ones out to the sea.

## Museo Diocesano de Arte Sacro

*Plaza de la Encarnación 9, T 944-320125. Tue-Sat 1030-1330, 1600-1900, Sun 1030-1330. Free. Metro: Casco Viejo. Map 1, E6, p247*

On a lovely cobbled square, this museum, set in a former monastery, features an attractive sunken cloister. The wide collection deals in a millennium's worth of religious art and artefacts, mostly taken from churches around Vizcaya. While many feel that the works should be *in situ*, it is a difficult endeavour to maintain and protect valuable artworks in near-deserted areas. The interesting pieces are accompanied by a rather sentimental

portrayals.

# The Riverbank

*You are, Nervión, the history of the town, you her past and her future,
you are memory always becoming hope.*
Miguel de Unamuno

*The Nervión river made Bilbao, and Bilbao almost killed the Nervión:
until pretty recently pollution levels were sky-high. Although your
immune system would still have words to say about taking a dip, the
change is noticeable. If you only take one stroll in Bilbao, an evening
paseo from the Casco Viejo along the river to the Guggenheim is it.*
▶▶ *See Sleeping p125, Eating and drinking p152, Bars and clubs p177,
Arts and entertainment p188*

## Mercado de la Ribera
Calle Ribera s/n, **T** 944-157086. *Metro: Casco Viejo.* Map 2, H3, p249

Built on the site where stallholders used to come for the weekly
market, this Art Deco riverside building is a permanent market of
ample size. With over 400 stalls on three floors of fruit, veggies,
meat and fish, it´s the major centre for fresh produce in Bilbao.
Come in the morning if you want to get the true flavour; the
afternoons are comparatively quiet. Skip the meat floor if you
don't want to see pigs' heads and horse butchers.

## Teatro Arriaga
Plaza del Arriaga 1, **T** 944-792036. *Metro: Casco Viejo.* Map 2, D12, p249

This large and ornate building sits just outside the Casco Viejo. On its
own block, and commanding the surrounding area, it seems very
sure of itself, but was only reopened in 1986, after decades of
neglect. Originally opened in 1890 with miraculous new electric
lighting, it was largely destroyed in a fire in 1915. It's in plush *fin de
siècle* theatre style, with chandeliers and sweeping staircases, but at

times presents some cutting-edge art. The theatre is named after Juan Crisóstomo de Arriaga, a Bilbaíno boy nicknamed "The Spanish Mozart" when he started dashing off octets before hitting puberty. He perished even younger than Mozart, dying in Paris in 1826, ten days short of his twentieth birthday.

## The Arenal
*Metro: Abando/Casco Viejo.*  Map 2, C12, p249

Between old town and new, this parky area is a focus of Bilbao community life: a busy nexus point for strollers, lovers, demonstrators and dogwalkers. Formerly an area of marshy sand, it was drained in the 18th century. There's a bandstand with frequent performances, often of folk dancing. From here, the **Puente del Arenal** crosses the Nervión to the new town.

## Café Boulevard
C Arenal 3, **T** 944-153128  *Metro: Abando/Casco Viejo.*  Map 2, D12, p249

Fans of Art Deco will not want to miss this refurbished defender of the style, unchanged from the early 20th century, when it was Bilbao's beloved 'meeting place'. Founded in 1871, it declined in parallel with the Teatro Arriaga opposite. Rejuvenated, it's now as vibrant as it was in the days of Unamuno, a regular here.

## Ayuntamiento
Plaza Ernesto Erkoreka.  *Metro: Casco Viejo.*  Map 2, A11, p249

The Ayuntamiento, or town hall, was built in 1892 and is an example of the new Baroque that was, alongside Art Nouveau, a reaction to the stifling artistic atmosphere that had prevailed in Spain for over a century. It's topped by a quirky little spire that's a bit out of place. It was designed by Joaquín de Rucoba, who was also responsible for the Teatro Arriaga that faces it down the river.

In front, by the river, is an intriguing sculpture by the controversial Jorge Oteiza. The evocative rusted-iron work, entitled *Ovoide de la Desocupación de la Esfera*, has been nicknamed *la txapela* ('the beret') by locals. Created in 1958, it was only recently installed here.

## ★ Zubizuri Footbridge
*Metro: Abando/Casco Viejo. Map 2, A8, p249*

Santiago Calatrava's bridges have won him world renown, and this is among his most graceful. Inaugurated in 1994, it was a powerful symbol of Bilbao's renewal before the Guggenheim was close to completion. Shining white in the sun like the ribs of some marine beast, it seems impossibly light. Although the footway is made of transparent glass, the Bilbao authorities have controversially covered it in non-slip plastic which blocks the view down to the water but prevents the less sure-of-foot from slipping into the river. The funky name of the structure means 'white bridge' in Euskara.

## Artxanda
*Funicular from Plaza Funicular, €0.50, runs Mon-Sat 0715-2200, Sun 0815-2200; summer until 2300, Sat/Sun. Map 2, A8, p248*

In a city enclosed by hills, there are sure to be some good vistas on offer, and one of the best is from the top of Monte Artxanda. Not far from the Zubizuri, a fire-engine red funicular rises to the top, a popular weekend gathering place for the burghers of Bilbao. There are a couple of places to eat, but if the day is nice a picnic is called for.

## Paseo Uribitarte
*Map 2, B7-11, p248*

This long riverside walk leading to the Guggenheim Museum is where plenty of Bilbaínos gather for the evening stroll, or *paseo*. Although the Nervión occasionally has problems with personal hygiene, Uribitarte is a lovely promenade that sometimes seems like the parade ground at a dog show as some seriously pampered pooches are brought out to take the city air.

## ★ Guggenheim Museum

Abandoibarra Etorbidea 2, **T** 944-359000, www.guggenheim-bilbao.es *Map 2, B6, p248 Tue-Sun 1000-2000, Jul/Aug only Mon-Sun 0900-2100. €7 admission, audio tour €3.61, guided tours free at 11.30, 1230, 1630, 1830 (Spanish, English, and Euskara depending on demand). Metro: Moyúa. Buses 13, 27, 38, 46, 48 stop a block away on Alameda Recalde.*

*"The idea was that the building had to be able to accommodate the biggest and heaviest of contemporary sculpture on the one hand, and a Picasso drawing on the other hand. In the first sketch I put a bunch of principles down, then I become self-critical of those images and those principles, and that evokes the next set of responses…and those evolve, and at some point I stop, because that's it."*
Frank Gehry

More than anything else, it is this building that has thrust Bilbao so firmly back on to the world stage. Daring in concept and brilliant in execution, it has driven a massive boom in the local confidence as well as, more prosaically, in the economy; its success has given the green light to further ambitious transformation of the formerly industrialised parts of the city.

It all started when the Guggenheim Foundation, strapped for cash (or something like that…), decided to build a new museum to enable more of its collection to be exhibited. Many cities around the globe were considered, but the Basque government was prepared to foot the US$100 million bill for its construction.

Frank Gehry was the man who won the design competition and his work is the reality of what confronts visitors to Bilbao today; a

**Best**

★ **Spots for a rainy day**

- Wine-tasting around Laguardia, p114.
- The Museo de Bellas Artes in Bilbao, p47.
- A waterfront bar in Lekeitio, p72.
- Sagardotegiak, p93.
- San Sebastián's new science museum, p94.

shining temple of a building that completely fulfils the maxim of "architecture as art". Gehry's masterstroke was to use titanium, an expensive soft metal normally reserved for Boeings and the like. Gehry was intrigued by its futuristic sheen and malleable qualities; the panels are literally paper-thin. The titanium makes the building shimmer and the impression is that the architect has managed to capture motion. The exuberant curves recall the shape of the fish, one of Gehry's favourite motifs; the structure could almost be a writhing school of herring or salmon.

One of the most impressive features of the design is the way it interacts with the city. One of Bilbao's most enjoyable experiences is to look up when crossing a street in the centre of town and see the Guggenheim framed by older buildings, like some unearthly vehicle that's just landed. Gehry had to contend with the ugly bulk of the Puente de la Salve running through the middle of his site, yet managed to incorporate the bridge fluidly into his plans. The raised tower at the museum's eastern end has no architectural purpose other than to link the building more effectively with the town upriver; it works.

The building also interacts fluidly with the river itself; the pool at the museum's feet almost seems part of the Nervión, and Fuyiko Nakaya's mist sculpture, when turned on, further blurs things. It's entitled *FOG*, which also happen to be the architect's initials…

A couple of creatures have escaped the confines of the gallery and live in the open air. Jeff Koons's giant floral sculpture, *Puppy*,

Demonstrators march through the streets of Bilbao's Casco Viejo, in silent protest against the treatment of Basque prisoners in Spanish and French jails. The ikurriña (Basque flag) flies proudly; the marchers carry photos of those imprisioned or killed by the authorities.

sits eagerly greeting visitors. Formerly a touring attraction visiting the city for the opening of the museum in 1997, he couldn't escape the clutches of the kitsch-hungry Bilbaínos, who demanded that he stayed put. On the other side of the building, a sinister spider-like creature guards the waterside approach. Entitled *Maman*, we can only be thankful that sculptor Louise Bourgeois' mother had long since passed away when it was created. It's a striking piece of work, and a bizarre sight when shrouded in mist.

What about the inside? It is, after all, an art museum. Gehry's idea was that there would be two types of gallery: "galleries for dead artists, which have classical [square or rectangular] shapes, and galleries for living artists, which have funny shapes, because they can fight back". The embodiment of the latter is Gallery 104, built with the realisation that many modern artworks were too big for traditional museums. Central to this space is Richard Serra's *Snake*, whose curved iron sheets will carry whispers from one end to the other. A hundred feet long, weighing 180 tons, it's interactive – walk through it, talk through it, touch it.

This, however, is one of only a few pieces that live in the museum; the rest are temporary visitors, some taken from the Permanent Collection of the Guggenheim Foundation, others appearing in a range of exhibitions; relecting the variation in quality.

Architecturally, the interior is a very soothing space with natural light flooding into the atrium. Jenny Holzer's accurately titled *Installation for Bilbao* is an arresting nine-column LED display, uniting the different levels of the building, and creating a torrent of primal human sentiment expressed simply in three languages.

There are three floors of galleries radiating off the central space, and a spot reserved for Picasso's *Guernica*, which the Basque government persistently tries to prise away from Madrid's Reina Sofia gallery.

For a look at smaller-scale Gehry work, drop into the reading room on the ground floor, furnished with his unique cardboard chairs and tables. The cafés also feature chairs designed by him. The museum has an excellent modern art bookshop and a souvenir shop.

## Palacio Euskalduna

C Abandoibarra 4, **T** 944-310310. *Metro: San Mamés.* *Map 2, F3, p248*

Opened in 1998 on the site of the last Bilbao shipyard, this bizarre building echoes both that industry and Vizcaya's iron trade. Awkwardly situated, hemmed in by a busy bypass, the structure leaves many people cold, although it is impressive in a clumsy kind of way. Particularly interesting are the coathanger-'trees' out the front. It's now a major venue for conferences and concerts, particularly classical.

● *More* simpático *is the covered* **Euskalduna bridge** *nearby, which sweeps into Deusto in a confident curve.*

Bilbao

# El Ensanche

*The residents of old Bilbao had long been crammed into the small Casco Viejo area when the boom came and the population began to surge. In 1876 the Plan de Ensanche (expansion) de Bilbao was approved, and the area across the river was drawn up into segments governed by the curve of the Nervión. The design drew on classical and Renaissance models, and it was felt that the hub of the new zone should be a large elliptical plaza. The Ensanche soon became Bilbao's business district, and today, its graceful avenues are lined with stately office buildings, prestige shops, and more than a few bars to adjourn to.*

▸▸ *See Sleeping p126, Eating and drinking p153, Bars and clubs p177, Arts and entertainment, p188*

## Plaza Circular

*Metro: Abando. Map 2, C11, p249*

Also called Plaza España (but not by Basques!), this is a busy focus of new-town goings-on. Bilbao's founder, Don Diego Lopéz de Haro, stands on a monument in the centre; he certainly wouldn't recognise his sleepy fishing village any more. Behind him looms the massive building of the Banco de Bilbao y Vizcaya, a skyscraper which can be strangely attractive as it reflects the sun. The main railway station, Abando, is just off the plaza, which is busy at all hours. One of Bilbao's most characterful cafés, *La Granja*, is on the north side; a good place for early evening drinking and snacking.

## Gran Vía Don Diego López de Haro
*Metro: Moyúa, Abando. Map 2, D10, p249*

Spanning the entire Ensanche, Bilbao's principal street starts at Plaza Circular. It's lined with banks and other important buildings, including the Palacio Foral, the seat of the Vizcayan government. There are many good examples of late 19th-century architecture; the imposing and sober bulk of some of them seems to define the work ethic that drove Bilbao's industrial boom. It's also a key shopping street with the massive *Corte Inglés* at one end, and a number of other boutiques. It's named after the founder of the town.

## Jardines de Albia
*Metro: Abando. Map 2, C10, p249*

A small, peaceful park in the heart of the business district, where employees of the adjacent law courts come to wind down. The headquarters of the PNV (Basque Nationalist Party) also face the gardens. There's a statue of the writer Antonio de Trueba at one end. He wrote poems, history and stories in a simple nostalgic style, very popular with his 19th-century public, and the Queen.

## Plaza Moyúa
*Metro: Moyúa. Map 2, E8, p249*

When the Ensanche was planned, the central focus was to be a plaza of oval shape; this busy meeting of eight streets is exactly what the planners had in mind. The inspiration for the formal garden in the centre came from France. The grand old *Hotel Carlton* keeps an eye over the square; this is where Ernest Hemingway used to lay down his grizzled head. He's one of a multitude of celebrities that have stayed here but, more poignantly, the hotel was the headquarters of the republican Basque government during the Civil War before it was forced into exile after the surrender of the city. Another interesting building on the plaza (which is sometimes named Elíptica) is the **Palacio Chávarri**, in intriguingly spiky Modernist style, which is used by the government.

### Museo de Bellas Artes de Bilbao

*Plaza del Museo 2, **T**944-396060. Tue-Sat 1000-2000, Sun 1000-1400, €4.50, €10 with Guggenheim (not exhibitions here though), €2 audio guide. Metro: Moyúa. Map 2, E6, p248*

Not to be outdone by its titanium colleague, the Museo de Bellas Artes has tried to keep up with the times by adding a modern building of its own to the existing museum. Opened in November 2001, the result is a harmonious credit to its architect, Luis Uriarte, who seamlessly and attractively fused new to old. The collection is a medley of modern (mostly Basque) art and older works – there's also a new space for temporary exhibitions. The Basque sculptors Eduardo Chillida and Jorge de Oteiza are well represented, in addition to avant-garde multimedia work by young artists. Among the portraits, the jutting jaw of the Habsburg kings is visible in two famous works. The first, of a young Philip II, is by the Dutchman Moro, the portrait of Philip IV, attributed to Velasquéz, and similar to his representation of the same king in the Prado, is a master work. The decline of Spain can be seen in the sad king's haunted but intelligent eyes, which seem to follow the viewer around the room. A lighter note is (perhaps unintentionally) struck by the anonymous *Temptations of St Anthony*, who is pestered by a trio of colourful demons.

### Parque de Doña Casilda de Iturrizar
*Metro: Moyúa, Map 2, E5, p248*

This wedge-shaped park provides a big dose of greenery to central Bilbao. It's a pretty, if slightly tired, retreat for a walk or a doze in the sun. There's a fountain surrounded by a very pretty colonnade draped with wisteria – it's a tranquil place which occasionally hosts open-air concerts in summer. Below, in the park's centre, is a pond with a desultory collection of depressed peacocks and waterfowl. On nice weekends the park fills with roaming families.

### El Metro
Greater Bilbao was in much need of an efficient public transport system when it commissioned Norman Foster to design an underground in 1988. In November 1995 the line was opened and the Bilbaínos were impressed with the Mancunian's work. Foster's design is simple, attractive and, above all, spacious; claustrophobes will be able to safely banish Bakerloo Line nightmares. Many of the stations are entered through *fosteritos*, distinctive transparent plastic tubes nicknamed for the architect; the station at **Sarriko** is dubbed *El Fosterazo* for its larger size.

### Calle Ercilla and Plaza Indautxu
*Metro: Moyúa, Indautxu. Map 2, H7, p249*

The pedestrianised part of Calle Ercilla tracks southwest from Plaza Moyúa and is yet another favoured spot for the *paseo*. It's one of Bilbao's premier shopping streets, with several high-class boutiques. The street ends at Plaza Indautxu, centre of the district of the same name, which is well stocked with bars.

> **!** Jeff Koons, creator of *Puppy*, see p41, was formerly married to Ilona Staller, better known as La Cicciolina, porn star, Italian politician, and subject of a *Pop Will Eat Itself* song.

## Plaza de Toros de Vista

C Martin Agüero 1, **T** 944-448698, **F** 944-102474.  *Mon-Fri 1030-1300, 1600-1800. €1.50. Metro: Indautxu.*   *Map 2, H10, p249*

Bilbao's temple of bullfighting sees most action during Semana Grande in August, when there are *corridas* all week. The locals are knowledgeable and demanding of their matadors, and the bulls they face are acknowledged to be among the most *bravo* in Spain. Tickets to the spectacles don't come cheap, starting at about €30 for the cheapest seats. Check the website for details of *corridas* and ticketing. The ring also hosts occasional concerts.

The bullring is also home to a museum dedicated to tauromachy; there are displays on the history of the practice, as well as memorabilia of famous matadors and bulls. It's one of the few museums open on a Monday, but it's closed at weekends.

## San Mamés

C Felipe Serrate s/n, **T** 944-411445.   *Metro: San Mamés.*  *Map 2, H3, p248*

Few in the world are the football teams with the social and political significance of Athletic Bilbao (see box, p210); support of the team is a religion, and this, their home stadium, is known as the 'Cathedral of Football'. Services are held fortnightly, usually on Sundays at about 1700. The Basque crowd are fervent but good-natured. Visiting fans from Spanish clubs will frequently try and wind up the home support by provocatively waving Spanish flags; the stadium usually gleefully bursts into a chant of *Españoles hijos de puta*, suggesting that Spanish mothers have a very old profession. This is an example of the Spanish football tradition of *morbo*, or the provocative rivalry between fans. It's well worth going to a game; it's a far more friendly and social scene than the average match in the rest of Europe. The Monday papers frequently devote ten pages or more to Athletic's game. Tickets for games usually go on sale at the ground two days before the game.

# Deusto

*On the right bank of the Nervión, just across the river from the Guggenheim and the Euskalduna concert hall, is the university barrio of Deusto. Frequented by artists, students and agitators, the cafés and bars hum with political discussion.*

▸▸ *See Sleeping p129, Eating and drinking p158, Bars and clubs p177, Arts and entertainment p188*

## Universidad de Deusto

Av de las Universidades 24, **T** 944-139000, **F** 944-139098. *Metro: Deusto. Map 2, B4, p248*

Bilbao's principal university was founded in 1886 by Jesuits, who felt that the Basque community needed a centre of learning. With a high academic standard, it now has over 20,000 students and staff.

The University has played an important role in Basque national-ism. After the civil war, Franco banned public universities from the Basque country, fearing they would breed opposition. Deusto remained, being privately run by the Jesuits, and became an impor-tant centre of radical opposition. Texts and music written in the Euskara language, still outlawed by Franco, circulated clandestinely on campus, and illegal lessons were given outside of class time.

The refined neo-classical main building, slightly downstream from the Guggenheim is the place to come for a postcard-perfect snap of Frank Gehry's masterpiece, particularly in the evening light.

## El Tigre

C Ribera Botica Vieja 23. *Metro: Deusto. Map 2, E2, p248*

One of Bilbao's most distinctive buildings, this was originally built as a pavilion to house the small workshops of local tradespeople. It was the first of quite a few of this type, some of which are still in operation along the Deusto riverbank. Topped with a huge stone lion, the other buildings are nowhere near as impressive. Now abandoned, the perversely named, El Tigre (the tiger) is due for conversion into luxury flats as Deusto inevitably becomes trendy.

### Iglesia de San Pedro de Deusto
Plaza de San Pedro.   *Metro: Deusto.*   *Map 2, D1, p248*

This 500-year-old building, in late Gothic style, is the parish church of Deusto. Despite its modern additions, this is a good example of a traditional Basque church, with its high triple nave and simple bell tower. The competent *retablo* depicting the life of St Peter is a Renaissance work by two Basque Martíns, Basabe and Ruíz.

## Around Bilbao

*At the mouth of the estuary of the Nervión, twenty-odd kilometres from Bilbao, the fashionable barrio of **Getxo** is linked by the improbably massive **Puente Vizcaya** with the grittier town of **Portugalete**, in its day a flourishing medieval port. Not far from Getxo stretch the languid beach suburbs of **Sopelana**, **Plentzia** and **Gorliz**; great stopovers, with plenty of restaurants and good hotels and campsites.*

▸▸ *See Sleeping p130, Eating and drinking p158, Bars and clubs, p175*

## Getxo

*Metro stops: Areeta, Gobela, Neguri, Aiboa, Algorta and Bidezabal; Buses 3411 and 3413 run from Plaza Moyúa every half-hour.*

Very much a separate town rather than a suburb of Bilbao, Getxo is a wealthy, sprawling district encompassing the eastern side of the rivermouth, a couple of beaches, and a petite old harbour. It's home to a good set of attractive stately mansions as well as a tiny but oh-so-pretty whitewashed old village around the now disused

*The charming lanes of Getxo's old port are complemented by good beaches, all handy on the Metro line. Just don't mention the word suburb to the locals, who regard Bilbao as the village upriver.*

fishing port-ette. There's a very relaxed feel about the place, perhaps born from a combination of the relaxed seaside air and a lack of anxiety about where the next meal's coming from.

## Playa de Ereagat
*Metro: Neguri.*

Ereagat is Getxo's principal stretch of sand, and the location of the town's finer hotels and general seaside life. In truth, it's an inferior beach; most of the view is taken up by the dockyards across the estuary while the distinctly black-tinged sand keeps many people back on the promenade. Still, it's an important social scene, and you haven't been to Getxo if you haven't strolled along its length, taking a coffee at one of the hotels.

## Puerto Viejo
*Metro: Algorta.*

The tiny harbour, now silted up, is a reminder of the days when Getxo made its living from fish. The solemn statues of a fisherman and a *sardinera* stand on the stairs that look over it, perhaps mystified at the lack of boats. Perching above, a densely packed knot of white houses and narrow lanes gives the little village a very Mediterranean feel, unless the sirimiri, the Bilbao drizzle, has put in an appearance. There are a couple of restaurants and bars to soak up the ambience of this area, which is Getxo's prettiest quarter.

## San Nicolás de Bari
*Metro: Algorta.*

At the top of the old port stands this attractive church. The stone is warm and rough-cut making it a building that you want to touch. A cool verandah runs around it, while the porch facing the square is used for impromptu *pelota* games by young locals. The church was built in the mid-19th century and is one of the friendlier examples of neo-classicism in the Basque Country.

## Playa de Arrigunaga
*Metro: Bidezabal*

Far more inviting than Getxo's main beach, this faces out to sea and hence avoids the estuary's pollution. Flanked by crumbly cliffs, it's got a more secluded feel too (except at weekends). Atop the cliff to the right is a surprising sight – an attractive 18th-century windmill in tip-top condition. Less protected than Ereaga, on some days the windmill has a better time of it than the shivering bathers.

## Walking down through Getxo
*Metro: Algorta*

Sturdy shoes fitted (Getxo's languid stretch is quite a distance), start from San Nicolás de Bari downhill along the pedestrian street Calle Basagoiti, making a detour (if you're in the mood) to the shopping areas to your left around Calle Telletxe. After briefly joining the main road, the pedestrian downhill stretch continues – a pretty avenue lined with what were once very swish mansions; a couple still are. One of the most striking is **Casa Rosada** ('pink house'), which no doubt won more accolades for its architecture than its name. At the end is the pointy **Iglesia de San Ignacio**, behind which stands the sturdier **Ayuntamiento** (town hall), built of Berango sandstone and featuring spirited arabesque ornamentation under its eaves. Descending the main road, Algortako Etorbidea, take the steep right down Calle Ereagako Jaispidea, turn left when you reach the beach. Rounding the headland past the marina, is **Casa de Náufragos**, built over the sea on arches, while on the landward side is an ostentatious series of 20th-century *palacios*.

Following the water along a lengthy promenade you'll reach the monument to **Churruca**, and a gardened mole stretching into the

### The Passionflower

*"It is better to be the widow of a hero than the wife of a coward".*
Dolores Ibárruri

One of the most prominent figures of the Spanish Civil War, Dolores Ibárruri, from the Bilbao suburb of Gallarta, near Portugalete, was known as La Pasionaria (the passion flower) for her inspirational public speaking.

Formerly a servant and a sardinera (sardine seller), she suffered grinding poverty, and the loss of two daughters in infancy but rose to prominence in the Communist Party in the 1930s, becoming a deputy in the parliament in 1936 (she was released from prison to take up her post). When the Civil War broke out, she became a powerful symbol of the defence of Madrid and the struggle against fascism as well as empowered womanhood. Straightforward, determined, and always dressed in black, she adopted the warcry "No pasarán" ("they shall not pass"),

which was taken up all over Republican Spain. She was instrumental in the recruitment and morale of anti-fascist soldiers, including the International Brigades. When the latter were withdrawn, she famously thanked them: "You can go proudly. You are history: You are legend. ....we shall not forget you". Ibárruri was never much involved in the plotting and infighting that plagued the Republican cause and was able to claim at the end of the war "I have neither blood nor gold upon my hands". When Franco was victorious in 1939, she flew to Russia, where she lived in Moscow. The dictator died in 1975, and, after 38 years, Ibárruri was re-elected to her old seat at the first elections in 1977. On her return to Spain the 82 year-old Pasionaria, still in black, proclaimed to a massive crowd "I said they shall not pass, and they haven't". She died in 1989.

estuary. Churruca was the engineer who channelled out this part of the waterway in the 19th century, making Bilbao accessible to large vessels; a vital step in its growth. The monument is in classic heroism-of-the-workers style; the man serenely watches two figures seemingly trying to crush each other under a slab of stone, symbolizing the struggle between earth and water.

Passing the hulking modern **Iglesia de Nuestra Señora de las Mercedes** (which contains highly-regarded frescoes) will bring you to the unmistakeable form of the **Puente Vizcaya** and the trendy shopping area of **Las Arenas** (Areeta).

### Puente Vizcaya

**T** 944-638854, www.puente-colgante.com   *1000-sunset. Crossings €0.24 per person, €1 per car, walkway €3. Metro: Areeta.*

A bizarre cross between a bridge and a ferry, the Puente Vizcaya, or Puente Colgante, (hanging bridge), was opened in 1893, a time when large steel structures were à la mode in Europe. Wanting to connect the estuary towns of Getxo and Portugalete by road, but not wanting to block the *ría* to shipping, the solution involved a 'gondola' suspended by cables from a high steel span. It's a fascinating piece of engineering – the modern gondola zooms back and forth with six cars plus foot passengers aboard. You can also ascend to the walkway 50 metres above. While it's not the Eiffel Tower experience the brochure suggests, it does provide good views.

### Portugalete

*Euskotren from Abando (Santurtzi line) every 12 mins weekdays, 20 mins at weekends; Metro: Areeta (across bridge); Bus 3152 from the Arenal bus station (Mon-Sat).*

On the other side of the Puente Vizcaya from Getxo is Portugalete, a solid working-class town with a significant seafaring history. In former times, before Churruca did his channelling work, the

Nervión estuary was a silty minefield of shoals, meanders and sandbars – a nightmare to navigate in anything larger than a rowing boat. Thus Bilbao was still a good few hours' journey by boat, and Portugalete's situation at the mouth of the *ría* gave it great importance as a port. Given its charter by Doña María Díaz de Haro, 'the Kind', it flourished as a whaling town and commercial port. Nowadays, although it looks thoroughly functional, it pre-serves a characterful old town and attractive waterfront strollway.

Above the waterside the old Casco is dominated by the **Iglesia of Santa María**, commissioned by Doña María the Kind at the time of the town's beginnings, although the current building, in Gothic style, dates from the early 16th century. There's a small museum inside. Next to it, the **Torre de Salazar** is what remains of the formidable compound built by Juan López de Salazar, a major landowner, in about 1380. The main living area was originally on the second floor – the first was a prison – and the tower was occupied until 1934; when a fire evicted the last residents. One of the Salazar family who lived here, Luís García, was one of the first chroniclers of Vizcaya. He had plenty of time to devote to his writings, as he spent the last few years of his life locked up by his loving sons.

On the other side of the Puente de Colgante, the **Muelle de Hierro**, built by Churruca, stretches north into the estuary.

---

### The beaches beyond
*Metro Larrabasterra, Sopelana, Plentzia*

Beyond Getxo a series of beaches, accessible by Metro, offer less crowded sunseeking and a variety of watersports and other activities (see p27). **Gorrondatxe** and **Barinatxe**, reached by walking from Larrabasterra metro, can feature some fairly have-a-go waves, and are the best surfing options on this stretch; the latter is nicknamed 'the wild beach'.

Further along, the strands of Sopelana and Plentzia/Gorliz, both with their own metro stops not far away, are more sedate, and good for escaping the crowds. Beyond the beach at Gorliz is some good walking along the jagged coastline.

## Castillo Butrón
Barrio Gatika s/n, **T** 94-6151110, **F** 94-6151525. *1030-2000 daily in summer, ring for winter opening.*

In the hinterlands behind Plentzia is a bizarre sight: the imposing bulk of a castle that would seem more at home in the Scottish Highlands or a Hollywood studio. Although the castle was the family home of the Butróns as far back as the 13th century, today's impressive structure was effectively constructed in medieval style in the late 1800s. Bristling with turrets and castellated beyond belief, it sits in a woody park signposted off the road between Getxo and Plentzia. Inside, a series of dummies reconstruct medieval life but it doesn't seem dank enough to really call the period to mind.

## Inland  61

Startlingly green hills interspersed with jagged peaks, between which nestle the most Basque of towns.

## The Basque Coastline  70

The rugged coast has excellent beaches and personable fishing towns that historically defined the Basque nation with the daring maritime expeditions.

## San Sebastián/Donostia  76

One of the peninsula's most beautiful cities, it's a place with a light and leisurely feel, and draws throngs of holidaymakers in summer.

## Vitoria/Gasteiz  98

While it lacks the big-city vitality of Bilbao or the languid beauty of San Sebastián it's a very satisfying city much-loved by most who visit it.

## Alava  107

The place to come for unspoiled nature, with spots of great natural beauty, and plenty of scope for hiking and other more specialized outdoor activities.

# Inland

"Too green to be Spain, and too rugged to be France", is how author Mark Kurlansky sees the Basque lands. The interior is just that. While picturesque **Oñati** and **Elorrio** meander along on past glories, **Gernika**, the symbol of Basque Nationalism, has moved on to be a thriving country town again. These towns and villages are a good place to experience Basque culture; the *baserri*, the sturdy stone farmhouse, is still the basic unit of rural life, and the centre of weekend social life is still the *frontón*, where pelota matches are fought out. Stumble across a fiesta, and you'll be astounded by the old-style contests: stone-lifting, woodchopping and sheep-wrestling. The interior is home to the ancient Basque religion; where pre-Christian deities inhabited the peaks, caves, and woods, outdoor sports are now a more common way of interacting with nature .

**Guipúzcoa** is crisscrossed by valleys which are lush from rainfall and dotted with small towns, some agricultural centres for the surrounding farmland, some seats of heavier Basque industry such as cement or paper manufacture. **Tolosa** and **Bergara** are typical of these, and have a proud history behind them. The valleys also conceal beautiful churches (as well as the massive **Loiola** basilica), and plenty of walks and picnic spots.

▸▸ *See Sleeping p131, Eating and drinking p160, Bars and clubs p181*

## ★ Guernica/Gernika

*Hourly trains from Bilbao's Atxuri station; buses half-hourly from C Hurtado de Amezaga in Bilbao, next to Abando station.*

"...the concentrated attack on Guernica was the greatest success", from a secret memo to Hitler written by Wolfgang von Richthofen, commander of the Condor Legion and cousin of the "Red Baron", First World War One flying ace.

A name that weighs heavy on the tongue, heavy with blood and atrocity, is Gernika. During the Spanish Civil War, in one of the most despicable planned acts of modern warfare, 59 German and Italian planes destroyed the town in a bombardment that lasted three gruelling hours. It was 26 April 1937, and market day in Gernika, which meant that thousands of villagers from the surrounding area were in the town, which had no air defences to call on. Three days earlier a similar bombardment had killed over 250 in the town of Durango, but the toll here was worse. Splinter and incendiary bombs were used for maximum impact, and fighters strafed fleeing people with machine guns. About 1650 people were killed.

Franco, the head of the Nationalist forces, simply denied that the event had occurred; he claimed that any damage done had been caused by Basque propagandists. Apologists for the man have since claimed that the German Condor Legion planned the attack without his knowledge. While there is no doubt that Hitler's forces were keen to experiment with this type of warfare, it is ridiculous to claim that Franco was not involved in the planning of an attack of this scale. In 1999 Germany formally apologized for the event; the Spanish remained conspicuous by their silence.

Although it was claimed by some that Gernika was a legitimate military target, this was not the case; in any event, no targets of military value were hit. Apart from a general wish to terrorize and subdue the Basque population, who were resisting the Nationalist advance on Bilbao, Gernika's symbolic value was important. For many centuries Basque assemblies had met here under an oak tree, attended by the monarch or a representative, who would solemnly swear to respect Basque rights and laws – the *fueros*. The town became a powerful symbol of Basque liberty and nationhood. The first modern Basque government, a product of the Civil War, was sworn in under the oak only six months before the bombing.

One of the most famous results of the bombing was Picasso's painting named after the town. " By means of it, I express my abhorrence of the race that sunk Spain in an ocean of pain and death".

Picasso had been commissioned by the Republican government to paint a mural for the World Fair, and this was the result. It currently sits in the Reina Sofia Gallery in Madrid, but Basque lobbying may bring it to Bilbao. A ceramic copy adorns a wall on Calle Allende Salazar.

Today, Gernika is anything but a sombre memorial. While it understandably lacks much of its original architecture, it's a happy and friendly place which merits a visit. Its Monday-morning market is still very much in business and entertaining to check out.

## Casa de Juntas

C Allende Salazar s/n. *1000-1400, 1600-1800 (winter), 1000-1400, 1600-1900 (summer). Free.*

Symbolically sited next to the famous oak tree, this building, since Basque semi-autonomy, is once again the seat of the Vizcayan parliament. The building's highlight is the massive stained-glass roof depicting the oak tree, which is outside by the porch. Part of an older trunk is enshrined in a silly little pavilion.

● *Behind the Casa de Juntas is the **Parque de los Pueblos de Europa**, which contains a sculpture by Henry Moore and one by Eduardo Chillida. Dedicated to peace, they recall the town's devastation.*

## Museo Gernika

Plaza Foru 1, **T** 94-6270213, **F** 94-6257542. *Mon-Sat 1000-1400, 1600-1900; Sun 1000-1400. No lunchtime closing in summer. Free.*

A comprehensive collection of documents about the Civil War and Gernika's role in it. There are many valuable descriptions from eye-witnesses, as well as recreations of the bombing. To place Gernika

**!** The Manic Street Preachers' song 'If you tolerate this' is inspired by anti-fascist posters from the Spanish Civil War. A picture of a child killed in the Gernika bombing accompanied the message: If you tolerate this your children will be next.

in context, there's a section on other cities destroyed by bombardment; the aerial assault here served as a template for similar raids in the Second World War and since. Chillida's sculpture in the **Parque de los Pueblos de Europa**, see above, is the subject of a multimedia display.

## La Reserva de Urdaibai

Gernika sits at the head of the estuary of the Oka river, a varied area of tidal sandflats and riverbank ecology that is home to a huge amount of wildlife. UNESCO declared it a Biosphere Reserve in 1984. It's a great spot for birdwatching, and mammals such as the badger, marten and wild boar are also present. The park headquarters (T 94-6257125) are just outside the town centre of Gernika in the Palacio de Udetxea on the road to Lumo. Vistas of the estuary can be had from either side, on the roads to Mundaka or Laida, but to really appreciate the area, you might be better off taking a tour (see Tours, p27).

## Cueva de Santamamiñe

*Bus from Gernika to Lekeitio (every two hours approx) can drop you at the turn-off just before the town of Kortezubi, a half-hour walk away. Hitching is easy. Tours are free but limited to 15 people on a first-come first-served basis. They run Mon-Fri at 1000, 1115, 1230, 1630 and 1715.*

Near Gernika, and well worth a visit, is the cave of Santamamiñe. It was an elegant and spacious home for thousands of generations of prehistoric folk, who decorated it with an important series of paintings depicting bison, among other animals. The chamber with the paintings is now closed to protect the 12, 000-year-old art from further deterioration. The cave itself is fascinating nonetheless, winding deep into the hillside and full of eerily beautiful rock formations. The cave is a short climb from the car park. The bar/restaurant at the bottom, **Lezika**, is a popular place for al fresco *cerveza*.

## Bosque Pintado

*Access daily. Free.*

Near the caves is an unusual artwork: the Bosque Pintado de Oma.
In a peaceful pine forest on a ridge, Agustín Ibarrola has painted
eyes, people and geometric figures on the tree trunks in bright,
bold colours. Some of the trees combine to form larger pictures –
these can be difficult to make out, and it doesn't help that most of
the display panels have been erased. Overall, it's a tranquil place
with the wind whispering through the pines, and there's a
strangely primal quality about the work.

A dirt road climbs three kilometres to the wood from opposite
the *Lezika* restaurant. It's accessible by car, but it's a nice walk.
If you are on foot, it's worth returning another way. Take the path
down the hill at the other end of the Bosque from the entrance.
After crossing a couple of fields, you'll find yourself in the tiny
hamlet of **Oma**, with attractive Basque farmhouses. Turning left
along the road will lead you back to the cave.

# Elorrio

*Bus from Bilbao bus station with Pesa 5 times a day.*

The most Basque of places, this inland Vizcayan community is
highly recommended for a peaceful overnight stay. Overlooked by
rugged peaks. There's a spirited Basque feeling about the place
with plenty of posters, flags and bars making the local position on
independence very clear.

The small and appealing old town is centred around the church,
its beautiful bell tower looks a treat floodlit at night. The church is
set on a shady plaza, also home to the **Ayuntamiento** (town hall),
which sports an old sundial and a couple of finger-wagging quotes
from the Bible. In the streets around the plaza are many

El País Vasco – Euskadi

well-preserved buildings. The attractive vine-swathed **Palacio de Zearsolo**, dates from the 17th century. Families of Elorrio must have been keen on a bit of one-upmanship – dozens of ornate coats-of-arms can be seen engraved on façades around the town.

Near the town, the **Capella de San Adrián de Argiñeta**, is surrounded by a set of tombstones that have baffled archaeologists. Carved from stone, they feature a series of apparently pagan inscriptions and designs. A more energetic walk is to climb the mountain of **Udalaitz/Udalatx** (1117m), the most distinctive of the peaks visible from the town. It's accessible off the BI632 about 7 kilometres from town, on the way to Mondragón, or, more easily, off the GI3551 outside of that town. The climb isn't as steep as it looks, but it's still a good workout.

## Markina

*Serviced by* Pesa *four times daily from Bilbao bus station (bus continues to Ondarroa), also by* Bizkaibus *every half-hour (slightly slower).*

This sunny village in the Vizcayan hills is set around a long leafy plaza. Not a great deal goes on here but what does is motivated by one thing and one thing only: *pelota*. Many *hijos de Markina* have achieved star status in the sport, and the *frontón* is proudly dubbed the 'university of pelota'. As well as the more common *pelota a mano*, there are regular games of *cesta punta*, in which a long wicker scoop is worn like a glove, adding some serious velocity to the ball play. Games are usually on a Sunday evening, but it's worth ringing the tourist office for details, or checking the website

The sandstone **Iglesia de Nuestra Señora del Carmen** is worth popping into for its typically ornate Baroque *retablos* (altarpieces). The hexagonal chapel of **San Miguel de Arretxmago** is a ten-minute stroll from the plaza on the other side of the river. Inside are three enormous rocks, naturally balanced, with an altar

★ **Postcard-pretty villages**

Best

- Laguardia, p114.
- Elorrio, p65.
- Getxo's old port, p53.
- Mundaka, p70.
- Hondarribia, p95.

to the saint underneath. According to local tradition, St Michael buried the devil here; a lingering odour of brimstone tends to confirm this. At midnight on September 29, the village gathers to perform two traditional dances, the *aurresku*, and the *mahai gaineko*.

### Museo de Simón Bolivar

C Beko 4, Bolibar, **T** 94-6164114, *Tue-Fri 1000-1300, Sat/Sun 1200-1400. Open 1700-1900 in Jul and Aug. Free.*

A half-hour walk from Markina, the hamlet of Bolibar features a museum dedicated to a man who never set foot here. Simón Bolivar, *El Libertador* (the Liberator) to half of South America, was born in Caracas to a family who originally came from here. The museum documents the family's history as well as the life and career of the man himself.

## Oñati

*Bus from Bilbao's bus station with Pesa once daily Mon-Fri, otherwise connect with local bus from Bergara.*

Oñati is one of the most attractive towns in the region with a proud history as a university town and, until the mid 19th century, as a semi-independent fief of the local lord. The **Universidad de Sancti Spiritus**, established in 1540, is a fine example of cultured

Renaissance architecture. The stately **Casa Consistorial** overlooks the main square where the two principal pedestrian streets, Calles Zaharra and Barria, meet to provide the focal point for the weekend nightlife.

## ★ Arantzazu

---

*No public transport from Oñati. Taxi costs about €10 each way. Walking from Oñati takes about 2 hours, but the return trip downhill is significantly less. There's plenty of traffic and it's easy to hitch a ride.*

---

Nine kilometres south of Oñati is the Franciscan sanctuary of Arantzazu, perching on a rock in a valley of great natural beauty. The basilica, built in the 1950s, is one of the most remarkable buildings in Euskadi. Incredibly avant-garde for its time, the spiky stone exterior is a reference to the hawthorn bush; according to tradition, a statue of Mary was found by a shepherd, led a tinkling cowbell, in 1468 on the spines of a hawthorn. The discovery ended years of war and famine in the area. The statue now sits above the altar, surrounded by the visionary abstract altarpiece of Luzio Muñoz. Although it appears to be made of stone, it's actually treated wood, and 600-metres square of it at that. The soft blue stained-glass windows add to the effect. Above the iron doors, sculpted by Eduardo Chillida, are Jorge Oteiza's fluid apostles and Pietá. He created great controversy by sculpting 14 apostles; for years they lay idle near the basilica as the Vatican wouldn't permit them to be erected. In the crypt, the impressive paintings of Néstor Basterretxea also caused problems with the church. He originally painted the crucifixion backwards; when this was censured, he repainted it, but with an angry Jesus. He succeeded – his powerful red Christ is now an imposing figure.

There are a couple of hotels and bars in Arantzazu but, happily, nothing else. There's some excellent walking to be done in the area, which is one of the most beautiful parts of Euskadi.

# Guipúzcoa's Central Valleys

## Sanctuario de Loiola/Loyola

*Bus: Pesa from Bilbao's bus station (3 a day), and La Guipúzcoana from San Sebastián's (destination for both is Azpeitia). Mon-Sun 1000-1300, 1500-1900.*

Now here's a strange one. A massive basilica, not quite St Peter's or St Paul's but not very far off, standing in the middle of Guipúzcoan pasture land. All is explained by the fact that St Ignatius, founder of the Jesuits, was born here. The house, where he first saw daylight, has bizarrely had the basilica complex built around it; it's now a museum. The most arresting feature of the basilica from a distance is the massive dome, which stands 65-metres high. Designed by Carlo Fontana, an Italian architect from Bernini's school, it's topped by an ornate cupola. Lavish is the word to describe the intricate decoration, best viewed from a distance, as the visitor approaches; Baroque haters and minimalist gurus will drop dead on the spot. Inside, the Baroque style verges on the pompous, with a silver-plated statue of Iñigo gazing serenely at elaborate stonework and marble. The best time to visit is during the week, as hordes of elderly pilgrims descend to pay their respects to the saint or the grandiosity of the building.

● *Those with a keen interest in the saint should head to the nearby Iglesia de San Sebastián in Azpeitia to see the font where he was baptized.*

## Museo Zumalacárregui

Ormaiztegi, **T** 943-889900. *Mon-Fri 1000-1300, 1500-1900; Sat/Sun 1100-1400, 1600-1900. Trains every half hour from San Sebastián (55 mins), buses from Bilbao to Tolosa stop here.*

In the small town of Ormaiztegi is the childhood home of Tomás Zumalacárregui, now a museum about him and the times he lived in. Fighting on the side of the pretender Don Carlos in the first

Carlist war, he gained an international reputation for his brilliant military victories and loyal guerilla army. He looked every bit the dashing romantic figure with a swashbuckling moustache and beret. Respected by the enemy, he won many battles in the early 1830s before being ordered to besiege Bilbao. The city held out, and Zumalacárregui was fatally wounded during the battle, dying aged 47. The museum includes documentation about both Carlist wars and 19th-century politics.

# The Basque Coastline

A brisk half-hour's walk is all that separates the fishing towns of **Bermeo** and **Mundaka**, but they couldn't be more different. Mundaka is petite and, these days, slightly upmarket as visitors come to admire its beautiful harbour. Bermeo puts it in the shade in fishing terms: one of the most important ports on this coast, there's a good atmosphere, and an attractive old town. On the other side of the Mundaka estuary The Basque Coastline continues unperturbed. After passing the beaches at the mouth of the ría, the land becomes rough-edged, with stirring cliffs and startling geological folding contrasted with green foliage. Fishing is god; some of the small villages are more accessible by sea than land. The major town, **Lekeitio**, is one of Euskadi's highlights.

▶▶ *See Sleeping p134, Eating and drinking p162, Bars and clubs p175*

## ★ Mundaka

*Hourly trains from Bilbao's Atxuri station*

While Mundaka still has its small fishing fleet, it's better known as a surfing village. It claims to have the longest left break in the world; whoever officially verified that had a pretty acceptable line of work. A left break is a wave that breaks from right to left, looking towards the beach. When the wind blows and the big waves roll in, a top surfer can jump in off the rocks by Mundaka harbour and ride a wave right across the estuary mouth to Laida beach, a couple of kilometres away. After the long paddle back it might not seem like such a good idea the next time. Apart from surfers, Mundaka gets its fair share of visitors attracted by its bonsai harbour and relaxed ambience. The village is a small maze of winding streets and an oversized church. There are some good places to stay or camp, and it's within striking distance of several highlights of the Basque coast. In summer, boats run across to **Laida beach**, which is the best in the area. It's almost worth a trip to see the *tigres* at the small bar on the estuary.

## Bermeo

*Bermeo is the last stop on the small train line from Bilbao Atxuri. Trains from Bilbao's Atxuri station hourly; buses half-hourly with* Bizkaibus *from the station next to the Bilbao main tourist office.*

Bermeo is a bigger and more typical Basque fishing town with a more self-sufficient feel. One of the whaling towns that more or less pioneered the activity, Bermeo has a proud maritime history which is documented in its museum.

There's much more action in the fishing harbour here than at peaceful Mundaka – boats are frequently coming and going, and there's some fairly good-natured jostling for position. There's a big *frontón* by the harbour; Bermeo likes to see itself as Vizcaya's number two sporting city and results sometimes bear them out.

The old town is worth wandering through. There's a cobbled square across which the church and the Ayuntamiento vie for power; the latter has a sundial on its face. There's a small chunk of the old town wall preserved, with a symbolic footprint of John the Baptist, who is said to have made Jonathan Edwards weep by jumping from here to the sanctuary of Gaztelugatxe in three steps.

**Museo del Pescador**
Plaza Torrontero 1, **T** 94-6881171, F 94-6186454. *Tue-Sat 1000-1330, 1600-1930; Sun 1000-1330. Free.*

Set in a 15th-century tower in the old part of Bermeo, overlooking the harbour, this museum is devoted to the Basque fishing industry. It gives a detailed history of all the ports on the Basque coast, has displays of the tools of the trade, and information about the various members of the finny tribes that have been fished through history.

● *The ships for Christopher Columbus' second voyage were built here, and many of the sailors were locals.*

# ★ San Juan de Gaztelugatxe

*Buses run from Bermeo (by the park on the harbour side) to Bakio every two hours along the coast road – San Juan is about 6 km from Bermeo.*

Sancho the Great, King of Navarra, was in Aquitaine, in France, in the early 11th century when a surprising gift was presented to the church hierarchy; the head of John the Baptist, which had mysteriously turned up a short while before. Understandably, the membership database of the cult of the Baptist received a boost, and many monasteries and sanctuaries were built in his name, including several in north-eastern Spain, with the express encouragement of the impressed Sancho.

San Juan de Gaztelugatxe is one of these (the church dates from much later). The setting is spectacular; a rocky island frequently rendered impressively bleak by coastal squalls, connected by a bridge to the mainland, and some 231 steps to the top. The island is a pilgrimage spot, particularly for the feast of St John on 24 June, and 31 July.

It's worth a look at **Ermito de San Pelaio**, a kilometre or so beyond (towards Bakio) the turn-off down to the island. This lovely 12th-century chapel overlooking a valley is attractively girdled by a

*The coast of Euskadi is rugged, rocky, and romantic. Tiny fishing villages cling to the rocks maintaining their ancient Basque livelihood.*

wooden verandah and is notable for its interior stonework. The church is only unlocked for services on Saturday from 1700 and Sundays at midday. There's a restaurant called *Ereperi* with a terrace overlooking the islet.

● *Bakio, 4 km away, towards Bilbao is a highly regarded beachside resort, although the reasonable beach is crowded by ugly development. There are a number of* txakolí *producers in the area; visits can be arranged through the tourist office.*

# Elantxobe

*Bus: Bizkaibus A3513 to Lekeitio stops in Elantxobe. It leaves Bilbao every two hours from Calle Hurtado Amezaga by Abando train station.*

If tiny fishing villages are your thing, Elantxobe might be worth adding to your itinerary. With amazingly steep and narrow streets leading down to a small harbour, it seems a forgotten place, tucked away at the bottom of a sheer escarpment. It's authentic without being overly picturesque.

# Lekeitio

*Bus: Bizkaibus hourly from Calle Hurtado Amezaga by Abando train station in Bilbao; Pesa four times daily from the bus station in San Sebastián.*

Along the Basque coastline, Lekeitio stands out as one of the best places to visit and stay. Its fully functioning fishing harbour is busy cheerfully painted boats, and old houses jostle and squeeze each other for a front-row seat. Once a favourite of holidaying royalty, the town is lively at weekends and in summer.

There are two beaches – the one across the bridge, is nicer. Both look over the pretty rocky **Isla de San Nicolás**, in the middle of the bay, home only to goats. The countryside around Lekeitio is beautiful, with rolling hills and jagged cliffs. The emerald green of the landscape doesn't come for free – the town gets its fair share of rainy days.

There's not a great deal to do in the town itself. The **Iglesia de Santa María de la Asunción** is definitely worth a visit. Lauded as one of the best examples of Basque Gothic architecture, it seems to change colour completely from dull grey to warm orange depending on the light. The *retablo* (altarpiece) is an impressive ornate piece of

Flemish work. If you ever wondered what a flying buttress was, take a look at the exterior. The narrow streets behind the harbour conceal some well preserved medieval buildings, while the harbour itself is lined with bars. Irish pubs claim a valuable victory over *McDonald's* by a slender 1-0 margin, but there are lots of traditional eating spots and inviting if pricey, accommodation options.

In a land of strange festivals, Lekeitio has one of the strangest, the *Fiesta de San Antolín* on 5 September. It involves a long rope, rowing boats, plenty of able-bodied young folk, and a goose. Thankfully, these days the goose is already dead. The hapless bird is tied in the middle of the rope, which is stretched across the harbour and held at both ends. Competitors take turns from rowing boats to grab the goose's head (liberally greased up) under their arm. The rope is tightened, lifting the grabber into the air, and then slackened. This is done until either the goose's head comes off, or the person falls into the water.

# ★ Ondarroa

*Bus: Pesa from Bilbao and San Sebastián bus stations four times a day.*

Although low on the glamour ladder and short on accommodation, Ondarroa is the friendliest of towns and could be worth a stop if you're exploring the coast, particularly at the weekend, when the nightlife rivals anywhere in the Basque Country.

Ondarroa is a centre of Basque nationalism, and if you're against the concept it might be worth not letting on. Music has long been a powerful vehicle of Basque expression, and here the bars pump not salsa or *bacalao* but nationalist rock. "*Bacalao* (salt cod) is for eating, not for listening to", according to one group of locals.

Ondarroa marks the border of Vizcaya and Guipúzcoa, and lies at the mouth of the Artibai river, straddled by two bridges. One, the harmonious **Puente Viejo**, the other a recent work of Santiago Calatrava, which sweeps across with unmistakable panache.

# San Sebastián/Donostia

The sweep of La Concha bay and the hills overlooking it draw inevitable comparisons for San Sebastián with Rio de Janeiro. The pedestrianized old town lies at the foot of the **Monte Urgull** hill, cheerfully and unabashedly devoted to tapas bars; the *pintxos* here are as good as anywhere. To the west is the fishing harbour, home to the **aquarium** and **naval museum**. The main beach stretches west to **Monte Igueldo**, the spot to head for holiday snaps with a panoramic postcard feel. The main business and shopping area, **Centro**, nestles between the beach and river in an orderly manner, while at the strand's western end is the secluded and exclusive barrio of **Ondarreta**. For a different feel, cross the river and wander around **Gros**, which keeps it real with good bars, a surf beach, and less pomp, except in autumn when the San Sebastián Film Festival hits town, taking place in its stunning **Kursaal** auditorium.

The green hills behind town, rolling like in an Irish ballad, are studded with villages which seem oblivious to the city's presence. This is where cider is made; in spring, people descend like locusts on the **cider houses** to drink it straight from the vat and eat enormous meals over sawdust floors. It's amazing any cider's left to be bottled.

▸▸ *See Sleeping p136, Eating and drinking p164, Bars and clubs p182, Arts and entertainment p189*

## Centro and New Town

*San Sebastián's refined new town defines the city's character in a sequence of elegant streets funnelled into the space between bay and river. Perhaps not surprisingly, there's more than a hint of France in the refined belle-époque façades and the stately sweep of the promenade around the beach. Although some of the glamour seems in need of a lick of paint, you still half expect to bump into María Cristina herself having a coffee and a pastry in a waterfront café. Fans of Art Nouveau will get sore necks wandering around these parts.*

## Playa de la Concha
*Map 4, E3, p245*

This beautiful curving strip of sand has made San Sebastián what it is.
Named after the *Concha* (shell) for its shape, it gets seriously crowded
in summer but is quiet at other times, when the chilly water makes
swimming a matter of bravado. Behind the beach, and even more
emblematic, is the Paseo, a promenade barely changed from the
golden age of seaside resorts. It's still the place to take the sea air
(so good for one's constitution) and is backed by gardens, a lovely old
merry-go-round, and desirable hotels and residences that still yearn for
the days when royalty strolled the shore every summer.

## Isla Santa Clara
*Transport: launch from El Muelle (summer only). Map 5, B2, p254*

This pretty rocky island could almost have been placed purposely as
a feature in the bay. There's nothing on it but a lighthouse and a
jetty, and it's only accessible by public transport during the summer,
when a motorlaunch  leaves from the harbour close to the end of the
beach. Its prime picnic territory with an unbeatable setting.

## Plaza Guipúzcoa
*Map 4, C5, p254*

An attractive shady green central park graces this important
square. On one side of the plaza is the **Diputación Foral**, while
the other side is the place to grab a bus to most destinations
within Guipúzcoa. In the park, there's a very manly statue of the
composer Usandizaga. Born in San Sebastián, he was a precocious
child who wrote his first waltz at the age of nine. His most famous
work was the extremely popular *Las Golondrinas* (The Wanderers),
a three-act *zarzuela* opera that catapulted him to stardom just
before his untimely death from consumption at 28.

## ▶ ETA and Basque nationalism

Although many Spaniards refuse to distinguish between them, Basque nationalism and ETA are very different things. The overwhelming majority of Basque nationalists are firmly committed to a peaceful and democratic path. ETA, pessimistic about the possibility of achieving these aims in this manner, seek by planned violence to force negotiation.

Culturally and ethnically distinct to Spaniards, Basques have a strong case for independence. The issue is muddied by the large number of Spaniards in the region, and the real sticking point is that Spain has no intention of giving up such a profitable part of the nation. Economics don't permit it, old-fashioned Spanish honour doesn't permit it, and, cleverly, the constitution doesn't permit it.

The nationalist movement was born in the late 19th century, fathered by Sabino Arana, a perceptive but unpleasant bigot and propagandist. He devised the *ikurriña* (Basque flag), coined terms such as Euskadi, and published independence manifestos peppered with dubious historical interpretations.

During the Civil War, the sundered Republic granted the Basques self-government; José Antonio Aguirre was installed as *lehendakari* (leader) at Gernika on October 7, 1936. An intelligent and noble figure, Aguirre and his government were forced into exile a few months later when Bilbao fell to Franco. Basques fought on in Spain and later in France against the Germans.

The birth of ETA is directly linked to the betrayal of this Basque government by the western powers. At the end of WWII, Republicans had hoped that a liberating invasion of Spain might ensue. It didn't, but Franco's government was ostracized and the Basque government-in-exile recognised as legitimate. But as the Cold War set in, America began to see anti-communist Franco's usefulness, and granted him a massive aid package. Following suit, France and Britain shamefully recognised the fascists and withdrew support from the horrified Basques.

ETA, which stands for *Euskadi Ta Askatasuna*, or Euskadi and Freedom, was founded by disillusioned youth shortly after this sordid political turnabout. Its original goal was to promote Basque culture in repressive Spain, but it soon took a violent edge. Their first assassination was in 1968, and they have killed over 800 since, mostly planned hits on rightist politicians, Basque 'collaborators' and police. The organization and uses extortion and donations to fund its activities. It currently demands autonomy for the Basque region, union with Navarra, and the transfer of all Basque prisoners to prisons within the region.

Despite the slogans, there's nothing noble or honourable about ETA's *modus operandi*. Many of the dead have little or no power within the régime; it often seems that the leadership has little control over its trigger-happy thugs. However, there's certainly an element of hypocrisy in the public attitude. In 1973, when an ETA car bomb killed Franco's right hand, Carrero Blanco, the group were liberationist heroes to many. Now, in cuddlier times, such actions are seen as appalling.

The authorities have foolishly been drawn into a cycle of violence. When ETA strike, their support drops dramatically in Euskadi, but there's often a violent police retaliatory action that causes anti-Madrid feeling to rise again. The Socialist government of the early 1990s scandalously funded a 'death squad' aimed at scaring Basques out of nationalism; Basque prisoners are routinely tortured in police cells. The escalationist attitude of Madrid continued in 2002, when they banned *Batasuna*, the political party widely seen as ETA's backers; surely not a step towards peace.

### Teatro Victoria Eugenia
Plaza de Oquendo s/n.  *Map 4, B5, p252*

This theatre, opened along with the *Hotel María Cristina* in 1912, was a similarly important icon of the social scene and hosted some of the world's leading artists during San Sebastián's golden period. It continued to be the city's major performing arts venue and home of the annual film festival until the opening of the *Kursaal* across the river. It's a beautiful building but is closed, for major restoration work until 2003, at the earliest. The small tourist train leaves from here hourly. The monument in the park opposite the theatre is to Oquendo, an admiral from a famous San Sebastián line of seadogs.

### Hotel María Cristina
Paseo Republica Argentina 4, **T** 943-424900, **F** 943-423914, www.westin.com  *Map 4, C5, p252*

Opened in 1912, this Belle Époque giant is one of the most opulent hotels in the whole peninsula. Taking up an entire city block with its elegant stone bulk, it looks across the river at the Kursaal the way an ageing society type might glare at a cheeky teenager. It's *the* place of choice for paparazzi and celebrity-stalkers; during the film festival all the big stars hang out here.

### Puente María Cristina
*Map 4, E6, p252*

This bridge over the Urumea river links the main railway station with the town. Opened in 1905, its lavish decorations endanger easily distracted motorists crossing it. An ornate tower stands at each corner, decorated with marine sculptures and the shields of city, province and country.

## Estadio de Anoeta

Paseo de Anoeta 1, **T** 943-462833, **F** 943-458941,
www.real-sociedad-sad.es  *Tickets €24-39 (sold at the stadium from
the Thu afternoon before a game to the Saturday evening, then 2 hrs
before the kickoff on Sunday). Map 5, H8, p254*

This is the home of Real Sociedad, the city's football team, given
the title *Real* (Royal) in 1910. The club is one of few to have won
the Spanish league title, which it managed twice running in 1981
and 1982.

● *Near the stadium is the brand new bullring, Illumbe, inaugurated in 1998 it includes a massive cinema complex. The city had been
without a bullring since 1973, when the famous El Chofe, in Gros, was
demolished.*

## Catedral del Buen Pastor

Plaza del Buen Pastor s/n.  *Map 4, E5, p252*

The simple and elegant neo-Gothic cathedral is lighter and less
oppressive than its older sidekick in the Parte Vieja, with an array of
geometric stained glass. In reality, there's little to detain the visitor
– it's more impressive outside than in. Students of poor-taste
works of art will, however, have a field day – the Christ with sheep
above the altar is upstaged by the painted choirboy with donation
box in hand.  Nearby, on Calle Arrasate, is a covered food market
that is busy in the mornings but not particularly impressive.

# Ondarreta

*Where the beach of La Concha graciously concedes defeat at a small
rock outcrop, the beach of Ondarreta begins. Behind it, streets of
tastefully wealthy mansions form an exclusive community overlooked
by the towering hill of **Monte Igueldo**.*

★ **Spots for people-watching**

Best

- Lezika beer garden near Gernika, p64.
- An outside table on Vitoria's Calle Dato or in the plaza, p101.
- A stroll along the Nervión between seven and eight in the evening, p37.
- La Concha beach and promenade in San Sebastián, p77.

## Palacio de Miramar

Paseo de Pío Baroja s/n. *Gardens open summer 1000-2030, winter 1000-1700. Map 5, D2, p254*

A rocky spur separates the beaches of La Concha and Ondarreta, which are joined by a natural tunnel. The rock is named the **Pico del Loro** after a long-forgotten chapel to Our Lady of Loreto. Atop it now is the Palacio Miramar. Commissioned by the regent María Cristina in the late 19th century,  it would not be out of place offering bed and breakfast in an English village. Built in Queen Anne style, its gardens have excellent views around the bay. The palace itself is closed to the public but is used by the university for summer schools.

## Playa de Ondarreta

*Bus number 16 from Plaza Guipúzcoa hourly/half-hourly in sumer, €0.80. Map 5, C2, p254*

The beach of Ondarreta gazes serenely across at the rest of San Sebastián from beyond the Palacio de Miramar. It's a fairly exclusive and genteel part of town, and is appropriately overwatched by a statue of a very regal Queen María Cristina. It can be a good place to stay in summer, with less hustle and bustle than the centre of town. The beach itself feels a bit more spacious than

## The Sculptors

You can't go far in the Basque lands without coming across a hauntingly contorted figure or sweep of rusted iron that signals a creation of Jorge de Oteiza or Eduardo Chillida. Their powerful work is emblematic of the region, but the product of two very different men.

Jorge de Oteiza, forthright and uncompromising well into his nineties, was born in Orio in 1908. After ditching a medical career in favour of sculpture, his big breakthrough came when commissioned to create pieces for the façade of the visionary monastery at Arantzazu in the early fifties. With his grey beard, beret and thick glasses, Oteiza cut quite a figure, but the anguish and power he channelled into his apostles and Pietá was extraordinary. The Vatican prevented the erection of the fourteen apostles for eighteen years. Oteiza has continued to strive, famously saying that "a monument will be no more than a pile of stones or a coil of wire if it does not contribute to the making of a better human being, if it is not…the moulded key to a new kind of man".

Eduardo Chillida, born in 1924 in San Sebastián, appeared between the sticks for *Real Sociedad* before a knee injury. A sculptor of world renown, the spaces he creates within his work are as important as the materials that comprise it. The *Peine de los Vientos* at San Sebastián and the *Plaza de los Fueros* in Vitoria are designed to interact dynamically with their setting, while his exploration of oxidised iron as a medium is particularly appropriate for Euskadi. His museum outside San Sebastián houses a cross-section of his massive output. Before his death, aged 78, in August 2002, the 'Man of Iron' was viewed as the world's greatest living sculptor.

On bitter terms for many years, with accusations of plagiarism from both sides, they finally buried the hatchet in 1997.

La Concha, not being densely backed by buildings. The amusingly old-fashioned **Royal Tennis Club** is at its western end.

## El Peine del Viento
*Bus number 16 from Plaza Guipúzcoa hourly/half hourly in sumer, €0.80.* Map 5, B1, p254

"The light of the Atlantic is a light that is mine; it's a dark light"
E. Chillida
    At the end of the Ondarreta beach the town gives way to the jagged rocky coastline of Guipúzcoa again. Integrating the two is El Peine del Viento, the Comb of the Wind, one of the late sculptor Eduardo Chillida's signature works. It consists of three twisted rusty iron whirls that at times do seem to be struggling to tame the ragged breezes that can sweep the bay. The paved viewing area was specially designed for the work and has a few airholes that can resonate with the sound of the sea or, in rougher weather, shoot spouts of seawater into the air.

## Monte Igueldo
*Bus number 16 from Plaza Guipúzcoa hourly/half hourly in sumer, €0.80. Funicular runs 1100-2000, €0.80/1.50 return. Park entry €1.10 (haphazardly applied).* Map 5, B1, p254

Above Ondarreta rises the steep Monte Igueldo, which commands excellent views of all that is San Sebastián. It's not a place to meditate serenely – the summit of the hill is capped by a luxury hotel and a slightly tacky funfair. But the view is special, and it's particularly unforgettable in the evening, when the city's lights spread out like a breaking wave below. The funicular runs up and

! Chillida asked to borrow helicopters from the US embassy to place the sculptures. They refused, and the sculptures were finally erected using a specially-designed floating bridge.

down from a station behind the tennis club at the end of the beach. Otherwise it's a walk up the winding road beside it.

# Parte Vieja

*The most lively part of San Sebastián is its old section, at the eastern end of the bay. Although most of it was destroyed by a fire during the Peninsular War in 1813 (one of several 'great fires' the city has endured), it's still very characterful, with a dense concentration of bars, pensiones, restaurants and shops. Protecting the narrow streets is the solid bulk of **Monte Urgull**, which shelters the small harbour.*

## Ayuntamiento
C Igentea 1, **T** 943-481000, **F** 943-426781.  www.donsnsn.es
*Map 4, C3, p252*

Built in 1881, the town hall was originally the centrepiece of the city's suave nightlife as a casino and concert hall. For forty years it hosted the famous and the fabulously wealthy and was a compulsory stop on the European high-society circuit until the dictator General Primo de Rivera claimed it for the government in 1923. Still an elegant focus of the town, it currently flies neither the Spanish nor the Basque flag; giving precedence to the former invites ETA attacks; the alternative is a rap over the knuckles from Madrid.

## El Muelle
*Map 4, C2, p252*

San Sebastián's small fishing and recreational harbour is a pleasant place to stroll. There's a handful of cafés and tourist shops, and you can see the fishermen working on their boats while their wives mend the nets by the water. Halfway round the harbour is a monument to **Aita Mari** (Father Mari), the nickname of a local boatman who became a hero for his fearless acts of rescue of other sailors in

fierce storms off the coast. In 1866 he perished in view of
thousands attempting yet another rescue in a terrible tempest.

### Museo Naval

Paseo del Muelle 24, **T** 943-430051, **F**943-431115, mnaval@kultura.
gipuzkoa.net *Descriptions in Spanish and Euskara. Tue-Sat 1000-1330,
1600-1930, Sun 1100-1400, €1.20. Map 4, B1, p252*

The harbourside museum succeeds in making a potentially intriguing subject slightly dry and lifeless. On the ground floor is an
exhibit of small boats and other accessories. Upstairs deals in the
maritime history of the area; San Sebastián's biggest moment as a
port was in the middle ages when it was an export centre for
Castilian wool and an important naval base. The city prospered in
the 18th century via the trade monopoly on South American chocolate established by the *Real Compañia Guipúzcoana de Caracas.*

### Aquarium

Plaza Carlos Blasco de Imaz s/n, **T** 943-440099, **F** 943-430092,
www.aquariumss.com *Tue-Thu 1000-1900 (2100 in summer),
Fri-Sun 1000-2000 (2200 in summer), €8, sharks fed at 1100 and
1600. Bar/restaurant and shop inside. Map 4, B1, p252*

What would a seaside resort be without an aquarium? San
Sebastián's isn't bad, although the entry fee is a little high. The
highlight is a massive tank brimming with finny things; fish, turtles
and rays, plus a couple of portly sharks to keep the rest of them
honest. There's a good perspex tunnel, which can also be viewed
from above. Apart from this, there aren't many other live
creautures, but there are decent displays on whaling and fishing,
temporary exhibitions, and the skeleton of a small whale that
greets arriving visitors. Viewing space can get crowded, particularly
at shark-feeding time, which isn't quite as dramatic as it sounds.

## Monte Urgull
*Fort; Mon-Sun 1100-1330, 1700-2000 summer only.*   *Map 4, A2, p252*

Not only does San Sebastián have a superb setting around the bay, it also lays on plenty of spots to climb up and appreciate the view. Monte Urgull, an important defensive position until the city walls were taken down in 1863, saw action from the 12th century onwards in several battles, wars and skirmishes. The hill is topped by a small fort, the **Castillo de la Mota**, once used as the residence of the town's *alcalde* and as a prison. It's got a small collection of old weapons, including a sword that belonged to the Moorish king Boabdil. There's also a large statue of Christ, the **Monumento al Sagrado Corazón**, which is not the only Rio-like aspect of San Sebastián. In summer there's a bar to quench your thirst after the 120-metre ascent. On the way up from the old town (there are many access paths) is the English cemetery. Plenty of soldiers died storming the town under General Graham after a siege in the Peninsular War in 1813. Graham defied conventional military wisdom, storming the breach in the walls at midday. He made up for his error by taking the unusual and risky step of firing his artillery over the heads of his troops and thus subduing the defenders. The valiant French garrison held out on this hill for another week after the town had fallen while the victorious British, Spanish and Portuguese pillaged the town, and setting it on fire; Calle 31 de Agosto was the only street to survive the blaze: its name is the date of the fire.

## Paseo Nuevo
*Map 4, A1, p252*

One of the city's nicest meanders can be had along this road encircling the bulk of Monte Urgull. It runs from the rivermouth around to the harbour and is particularly enjoyable in the evening, when the sun sets over the sea. The road dead-ends for cars at the Aquarium and is accessed from Paseo de Salamanca on the river.

> ## Gastronomy in San Sebastián

Eating is a large part of life throughout the Basque country, but San Sebastián is the food capital, perhaps because people have more time and cash on their hands. Several of the best restaurants in the business are in and around town, and modern Guipúzcoan chefs make waves worldwide.

A more unusual aspect is the *txokos*, or gastronomic societies, whose spiritual home is Donostia. Most are private clubs with an all-male membership. The three key parts of a *txoko* are a members' lounge, a dining room, and a vast kitchen. The members gather to swap recipes and prepare massive gourmet meals to be devoured by themselves, friends, and family. It's invitation only (also see Tours, p27); if you want in, the best bet look around San Sebastián and make friends with tubby men with a twinkle in their eye.

A more accessible scene is the *sagardotegiak* (cider houses) that speckle the hills south of tow, see p93.

### Iglesia de Santa María del Coro
C 31 de Agosto s/n. *Map 4, B3, p252*

With a façade about as ornate as Spanish Baroque ever got, the church of Santa María del Coro squats under the rocks of Monte Urgull and faces the newer cathedral across the city. After the exuberant exterior, the interior can seem a bit oppressive with its low lighting, heavy oil paintings, and the numbing scent of incense. Above the altar is a large depiction of the man the city was named after, unkindly known by some as the 'pincushion saint' for the painful way he was martyred. Facing him is a stone crucifix in the unmistakeable style of Eduardo Chillida.

## Museo de San Telmo

Plaza Zuloaga 1, **T** 943-424970, **F** 943-430693. *Tue-Sat 1030-1330, 1600-1930, Sun 1030-1400. Free. Map 4, A4, p252*

This museum, set in a 16th-century Dominican convent, is worth a visit if only for its perfect Renaissance cloister. The ground floor of the museum houses temporary exhibitions, and a series of grave markers paired with evocative poetic quotes on death. Upstairs is devoted to painting and sculpture. Fittingly, as the museum sits on a square named after him, Ignacio Zuloaga is well represented. He was a worthy sucessor to the likes of Velazquéz and Goya in the art of portrait painting, and one of the best examples here is his deep and soulful Columbus (far more Basque than Genoan...).

● *There's a small memorial to Zuloaga in the plaza. If you like his work, there is a Zuloaga museum at Zumaia, see p97.*

## Iglesia de San Vicente

C San Vicente s/n. *Map 4, A4, p252*

The most interesting of San Sebastián's churches, this castle-like sandstone building squats in the northeast of the Parte Vieja. Started in the early 16th century, it features a massive *retablo* with various biblical scenes. More gracious is Oteiza's fluid modern **Pietá** outside the southern door of the church.

## Plaza de la Constitución

*Map 4, B4, p252*

This attractive porticoed square once served as a bullring and the balconies were sold off as seats: the numbers have been kept as a nod to history. There's some good eating to be had in some of the bars around the square. When the French occupied the town in 1794 they set up a guillotine in the square's predecessor, but only two people ever felt the Madame's kiss. Nowadays, the square is the focus of some of the city's happier events, such as the *Tamborrada* drum parade on 19 January, see Festivals p195.

### La Brecha
*Map 4, B4-5, p252*

This underground food market, cinema and shopping complex, built on the site of the old market, uses the original building of La Brecha. The town walls ran along this spot; in the siege of San Sebastián the British artillery destroyed them at this point, and anti-Napoleon forces poured through, after suffering heavy casualties – *Brecha* is the Spanish for 'breach'. Opposite is **Plaza Sarriegui**, where there is a monument to the composer of the same name who wrote the *San Sebastián March*, a series of drum scores, deafeningly rendered for 24 hours during the Tamborrada, see Festivals p195.

## Gros

*A bit more down-to-earth and relaxed than the rest of the town, Gros lies across the river and backs a good beach which sees some decent surf. Formerly a bit of a backwater as society strolled along La Concha beach on the other side of town, Gros is now firmly in the spotlight, with the unmistakeable **Kursaal** dominating its shoreline and film festival celebrities sunning themselves outside. Delving a bit further will unearth some great pintxo bars and some friendly attitudes.The heart of Gros is centred around the open square of **Plaza de Cataluña**, which contains the slender neo-gothic **Iglesia de San Ignácio**.Within a couple of blocks there are many excellent pintxo bars.*

### Kursaal
Av Zurriola 1, **T** 943-003000, **F** 943-003001, www.kursaal.org *Guided tours €2 at 1330 weekdays, weekends 1130, 1230, 1330. Tickets for events can be obtained at the box office or by phone.* *Map 4, A6, p252*

In a space derelict for three decades since the old Kursaal was demolished, these two stunning glass prisms opened their doors in 1999. Designed by Navarran architect Rafael Moneo to harmonize with the rivermouth and the sea, and 'communicate' with the hills of Uría and Urgull, the concert hall has inspired much comment. The architect fondly refers to his building as "two stranded rocks" – critics might agree – but the overall reaction has been very positive, and in 2001 the building won the European Union prize for contemporary architecture. The Kursaal looks at its most impressive when reflecting the setting sun, or when lit up eerily at night.The main building hosts concerts and conventions, while its smaller sidekick is an attractive exhibition centre. It's the new home of the San Sebastián Film Festival.

## Playa de la Zurriola
*Buses 8, 13, 14, 17.   Map 4, A7, p252*

Unlike the fairly sheltered bay of La Concha, the beach at Gros faces the open sea and gets some good waves. It was dangerous for swimming until the massive breakwater was built to pacify the currents and filter off pollution. The structure extends for a kilometre, much of it submerged. This is the best place for surfing, and there are plenty of shops around catering to the religion.

## Plaza del Chofre
*Map 4, B8, p252*

The most important thing about this small park is what is no longer there. El Chofre was one of the greatest of bullrings, and old-timers still swear that the sport has never been the same since its demise. Inaugurated in 1903, it was named after a farm that had stood on this spot. Hemingway describes how it was an essential part of the social scene, even for those who didn't care for it:

"By buying any sort of seat within diving range of the barrera at San Sebastián you could be sure of having a hundred-peseta seat to occupy when the citizens who knew they were morally bound to leave the bullring after the first bull stood up...They could go to the bullfight, but they had to meet at the Casino after they had seen the first bull killed. If they didn't leave and liked it there was something wrong with them. Maybe they were queer. There was never anything wrong with them. They always left. That was until bullfights became respectable".

El Chofre was demolished in 1973 after political pressure from developers and public apathy. The city lasted for a quarter of a century without a bullring until a new one was built near the football stadium.

## Monte Ulía
*Access by car on Paseo de Ulía off Avenida de Ategorrieta 3 km east of the river.*

The easternmost of San Sebastián's three hills offers predictably excellent views, and can be climbed from the eastern end of Zurriola beach. There's plenty of space for a picnic at the top, and there's also a decent restaurant.

## The Riverbank and the Parque Cristina Enea
*Map 4, G7, p252*

The Gros side of the River Urumea makes a nice wander; there are very characterful old mansions on the bank, and good views across to the **Hotel María Cristina** and the theatre. If you pass over the tracks at the railway station you'll get to the Cristina Enea park, a small palace with rambling grounds that were left to the city by the Duke of Mandas in the early 20th century. Due to the Duke's eccentric will, the park has barely been touched since his death. With its ambitious remodelling plan it should soon be revitalized.

# Southern Hills

*Only a few kilometres from the fashionable Donostian beaches, the city gives way to green hills. Much of the immediate area is devoted to **cider production**. **Chillida's sculpture park** and the new **Science Museum** are two more reasons to tear yourself away from the seaside.*

## The Cider Houses

Around Hernani and Astigarraga, www.sagardotegiak.com   *Buses from Plaza Guipúzcoa.*

Although it's not hugely popular as a day-to-day drink in San Sebastián these days, cider has an important place in Guipúzcoan history. It's nothing like your commercial ciders, being sharpish, yeasty and not very fizzy. It's best drunk fresh and has to be poured from a height to give it some bounce after hitting the glass. The cider is mostly made in the hills near San Sebastián in a great number of small *sagardotegiak*, or *sidrerías* (cider houses). When it's ready, in early January, these places dust down the tables, and fling the doors open to the Donostian hordes, who spend whole afternoons eating massive traditional cider-house meals and serving themselves freely from taps on the side of the vats. Tradition has it that this lasts until late April or so, although several places are now open year-round. The typical meal starts with *tortilla de bacalao* (salt-cod omelette), continues with a massive slab of grilled ox, and concludes with cheese, walnuts, and *membrillo* (quince jelly). The best of the places are the simpler rustic affairs with long shared rowdy wooden tables and floors awash with the apple brew, but these tend to be harder to get to. Expect to pay from €15-30 for the *menú sidrería*, which includes as much cider as you feel like sticking away. The tourist office in San Sebastián has a map and list of the cider houses; several are in very picturesque locations, and there are several walking trails through the hills and valleys from Astigarraga and Hernani, a 15-minute bus ride from the centre of San Sebastián.

### Kutxaespacio de la Ciencia

Paseo Mikeletegi 43, **T** 943-308211, **F** 943-308240,
www.miramon. org *Oct-May Tue-Sat 1000-1900, Sun 1100-1900;*
*Jun-Sep Tue-Sat 1000-2000, Sun 1100-2000. €5. Planetarium*
*sessions: 6-7 multilingual daily, €2, reservations* **T** *943-012476.*
*Bus 28 leaves hourly, approx, from Alameda del Boulevard.*

This brand-new bank-sponsored science museum looks appropriately futuristic with an off-kilter tower writhing into the air on the
southern outskirts of the city. There are plenty of good interactive
displays as well as temporary exhibitions on the natural world, the
body, the earth and technology. There's even a planetarium with a
good stargazing show. Very popular with school groups midweek.

### Museo Chillida-Leku

Bº Jauregui 66, **T** 943-336006. *1000-1500 Wed-Mon (Jul/Aug to 1900).*
*Bus 92 from C Oquendo every 30 mins on the half-hour.*

A very relaxing place to spend a few hours out of the city. Before
his death in August 2002, Chillida, the late Basque sculptor (see
box, p83.) gracefully restored this 16th-century farmhouse with his
own concepts of angles and open interior space. The lower floor
has a selection of large pieces; upstairs houses some of his earlier
work, as well as preparatory drawings. Surrounding the house is a
peaceful park, where around 40 of his sculptures are displayed; the
organized should pack a picnic.

## East of San Sebastián

*Although France is but a few kilometres away, the last stretches of Spain*
*are well worth investigating. The ancient port of **Pasaia** is seriously*
*industrial, but preserves a picturesque old port. East of here, the GI3440*
*rises steeply towards the east, resulting in fantastic views over a long*
*stretch of coastline; it's well worth going this way if you can.*

***Hondarribia**, the last town in Spain (or the first, to the healthy number of tourists entering from France), is a very beautiful walled town free of the malaise that afflicts most border towns; if you don't mind a few day-trippers, this is one of the most agreeable towns in Euskadi.*

## Pasajes/Pasaia
*Bus from Plaza Guipúzcoa, San Sebastián every 20 mins Mon-Sat (30 mins Sun),operated by Herri Bus.*

Pasajes is the name given to the towns that cluster around a superb natural harbour six kilometres east of San Sebastián. **Pasajes San Juán** (Pasai Donibane), distinct fromthe other parts that are devoted to large-scale shipbuilding, makes a very good trip out of the city. It's a charming town whose one street, wends its way along the water, winding around some buildings and simply going through others. Now dwarfed by the industry across the water, it was for periods in history the most important Basque port. Pasajes gets a few French tourists strolling through, which means that there are some good restaurants. Apart from eating and strolling, there's not much on, although you could investigate *Ontziola* (T 943-494521), an organization that builds traditional Basque boats.

## Hondarribia/Fuenterrabia
*Buses from Plaza Guipúzcoa in San Sebastián every 20 mins.*

This old fishing port sits at the mouth of the River Bidasoa looking directly across at France, a good deal more amicably now than for much of its history. The well-preserved 15th-century walls weren't erected just for decoration, and the city has been besieged more times than it cares to remember. The **Isla de los Faisanes** (Isle of Pheasants) in the middle of the river was considered suitably neutral ground for a peace settlement between the two countries in 1659, while Franco went one step further during the Second World War and met Hitler in Hendaye, just across the river.

Although there's a fishing port and a decent beach, the most charming feature of Hondarribia is the walled part, a hilly grid of cobbled streets entered through arched gates. The stone used for many of the venerable old buildings seems to be almost luminous in the evening sun. The hill is topped by a plaza and a 16th-century palace of Charles V, now a *parador*. Near by, the **Iglesia Santa María de Manzano** is topped by a bell-tower and an impressive coat-of-arms. **Plaza Guipúzcoa** is even nicer than the main square, with cobbles and a small but ornate buildings overhanging a wooden colonnade. There are nice walks around the river and in the hills above, including some marked trails, details from the tourist office. The town is also notable for its excellent restaurants; the standard no doubt kept high by the visiting French.

# West of San Sebastián

*The Guipúzcoan coast west of San Sebastián is characterized by some fairly muscly cliffs placated by a few excellent beaches. As with Vizcaya, the area's history is solidly based on the fishing of anything and everything, from anchovies to whales. **Getaria** is the most characterful of the towns along this stretch, but for a bit more action you might want to check out **Zarautz**, which becomes a busily upmarket beach resort during holiday season.*

### Getaria/Guetaria
*Bus from San Sebastián bus station with Euskotren.*

Improbably perched on a hunk of angled slate, Getaria is well worth a stop en route between Bilbao and San Sebastián. Despite being a large-scale fish cannery, the town is picturesque, with cobbled streets winding their way to the harbour and, bizarrely, through an arch in the side of the church.

Getaria gets its fair share of passing tourists, reflected in the number of *asadors* that line its harbour and old centre. For an unbeatable authentic feed, grab a bottle of sprightly local *txakoli* and wash it down with a plate of grilled sardines.

The **Iglesia de San Salvador**, is intriguing. The wooden floor lists at an alarming angle; to the faithful in the pews the priest seems to be saying mass from on high.

You won't stay long without coming across a statue of **Juan Sebastián Elkano**, winner of Getaria's most famous citizen award for 480 years running, although fashion designer Cristobal Balenciaga has come close in recent times. Elkano, who set sail in 1519 on an expedition captained by Magellan, took command after the skipper was murdered in the Philippines. Sailing into Seville with the scant remnants of the expedition's crew, he became the first to circumnavigate the world. Not a bad finish for someone who had mutinied against the captain only a few months after leaving port.

Beyond the harbour, the wooded hump of **San Antón** is better known as *El Ratón* (the mouse), and it certainly does resemble that rodent. There are good views from the lighthouse at its tip; on a clear day you can see the coast of France on the horizon.

---

★ **Museo Ignacio Zuloaga**

Carretera San Sebastián-Bilbao, Zumaia, **T** 943-862341, **F** 943-862512. *Wed-Sun 1600-2000 Apr-Sep only. Zumaia is serviced by Euskotren hourly from Bilbao's Atxuri station and San Sebastián's Amara station, also regularly by bus from San Sebastián bus station. It's a 15-min walk on the Getaria/San Sebastián road from the centre of Zumaia.*

---

Five kilometres to the west of Getaria is the town of Zumaia, at the mouth of the river Urola. The major attraction is the Zuloaga museum just to the east of town. Ignacio Zuloaga, born in 1870, was a prominent Basque painter and a member of the so-called "Generation of '98", a group of artists and thinkers who symbolized Spain's intellectual revival in the wake of the loss of the Spanish-American

War, known as "the disaster". Zuloaga lived in this pretty house and garden, which now contains a good portion of his work as well as other paintings he owned, including Goyas, El Greco, Zurbarán and others.

Zuloaga is most admired for his expressive portraiture, with subjects frequently depicted against a bleak Spanish landscape. In his best work, the faces have a deep wisdom and sadness that seems to convey both the artist's love and hatred for his country.

### Zarautz

In the absence of constructive parental guidance, the aim in life of Zarautz seems to be to try and outdo its big brother Sebastián just along the coast. Similarly blessed with a beautiful stretch of sandy beach and a characterful old town, Zarautz has suffered from quick-buck beachfront high-rise development. Despite the rows of bronzed bodies and the prudish but colourful changing tents, it can be quite a fun place. There's a good long break for surfing – one of the rounds of the world championship is often held here, and there's scope for more unusual water sports such as windboarding. There are a few well-preserved mediaeval structures, such as the **Torre Luzea**, and a handful of decent bars. Zarautz is also known for its selection of classy restaurants; after all, there's more to a Basque beach holiday than fish 'n'chips.

# ★ Vitoria/Gasteiz

It comes as a surprise to many to find out that the capital of the Basque semi-autonomous region is untouristed Vitoria. Less glamorous than San Sebastián and less metropolitan than Bilbao, it's a likeable place, full of green spaces and chatting students.

The city's outskirts are a little strange, circled with large homogeneous apartment blocks suitably interspersed with parks to keep the "quality of life" statistics high. The Casco Antiguo is much more charming, if a little run-down in places. As usual it's the focus of much of the city's nightlife, especially on Calle Cuchillería at weekends. The Ensanche is attractive too, with an excellent city park and a number of musuems, most notably the new Artium. Vitoria's most charming architecture is where the two areas meet, with the arcaded Plaza de España and the curious Arquillos, designed to integrate the higher old town with the low spread of the new.

▸▸ *See Sleeping p143, Eating and drinking p169, Bars and clubs p185, Art and entertainment p189*

## Ensanche

*Vitoria's new town isn't going to blow anyone's mind with a cavalcade of Gaudí-esque buildings or wild street parties but it is a very satisfying place: a planned mixture of attractive streets and plenty of parkland. It's got the highest amount of greenery per citizen of any city in the country and it's no surprise that it's been voted one of the best places to live in Spain. With the innovative Artium now in place, the mantle of 'Basque capital' seems to sit ever easier on Vitoria's shoulders.*

---

**Artium**
C Francia 24, **T** 945-209020, **F** 945-209049, www.artium.org
*Tue-Fri 1100-2000, Sat/Sun 1030-2000. €3. Wed "you decide".*

---

The shiny new Artium (opened April 2002) is Vitoria's answer to Bilbao's Guggenheim and San Sebastián's Kursaal. An exciting project, it features excellent contemporary artwork and many exhibitions, which incorporate some of the older buildings in Vitoria's Casco Medieval. The visitor's attention is taken immediately by the confident angles of the building and *Un pedazo de cielo cristalizado* (A crystallized piece of heaven) by Javier Pérez, a massive hanging glass sculpture in the atrium. The work by contemporary artists, mostly Basque, is backed up by some earlier 20th-century pieces by Miró, Dalí and Picasso, among others. There is a cool little café.

*Opened in April 2002, the clean white lines of Vitoria's Artium house an excellent collection of modern art appropriate for the educated and elegant Basque capital.*

### Plaza de los Fueros

This strange sunken triangle is the work of Eduardo Chillida, designed to commemorate the timeless Basque *fueros*, or statutes, which are still very much the groundstone of the separatist position. There's a frontón in one corner where you have a reasonable chance of seeing a game of pelota. Otherwise, it's a place to sit on steps and chat, smoke or contemplate as folk in a hurry stride past.

On C Prudencio María Verástegui 14, **Segunda Mano**, is an amazing second-hand shop which literally seems to have everything, from skis, to confessionals, to tractors.

### Calle Eduardo Dato

The new town's nicest street, pedestrianized and stretching from the old town to the railway station, is the focus of the knock-off-time scene, with a hatful of excellent cafés and bars where people cheerfully munch *pintxos* to stave off the pangs until dinner. The street is further enhanced by a couple of characterful sculptures.

### Catedral de María Inmaculada

C Cadena y Eleta s/n, **T** 945-150631. *Museum Tue-Fri 1000-1400, 1600-1830; Sat 1000-1400; Sun 1100-1400. Free.*

There's no missing the New Cathedral, built in the 20th century in neo-Gothic style; it's bulk looms attractively over this part of town. Built in authentic medieval style, it now houses the **Museo Diocesano de Arte Sacro** in its large apse. This has a good collection of religious art and has succeeded in bringing excellent temporary exhibitions to supplement it since opening in 1999.

### Parque de la Florida

This gorgeous park is an excellent retreat right in the heart of Vitoria. Cool and shady, it has a number of exotic trees and plants and a couple of peaceful cafés. You can watch old men in berets playing *bolas* (boules), and there's an old bandstand with Sunday concerts, guarded by statues of four ancient kings. If you see anyone taking things too seriously, they're probably politicians - the Basque Parliament stands in one corner of the park.

### Museo de Bellas Artes

Paseo Fray Francisco 8, **T** 945-181918, **F** 945-181919. *Tue-Fri 1000-1400, 1600-1830; Sat 1000-1400; Sun 1100-1400. Free.*

Located in a very grand 20th-century palace, this art museum has lost some of its more interesting work to the new Artium. It still has a good collection of Basque art, including canvases by Zuloaga, as

## The Bridgebuilder

Santiago Calatrava (born 1951) is well-equipped for his work, having first studied architecture in his native Valencia, then civil engineering in Zürich. From this grounding he has risen to become one of the most inspiring designers in the world, famous above all for the beauty of his bridges.

In the hurry to rebuild demolished bridges after the wars of the twentieth century, aesthetic concerns were understandably forgotten, but Calatrava feels that they are of vital importance. "I am a believer in attempting to change, in a very small measure, the quality of life. Your bridges can be better, your schools can be better, your public transportation – your *everyday life* can be better". He is intrigued by the basic human need of getting from one place to another, and has focused most of his work to this end: bridges, airports, railway stations.

Calatrava uses quite simple, classical principles and natural forms; his works seem to capture movement and enhance space. He has been very busy in Euskal Herria in recent years, designing the Zubuzuri bridge, airport, and control tower in Bilbao, a bridge in Ondarroa, and the Ysios winery just outside of Laguardia.

well as some Flemish masters, and a decent selection of coins. The formal garden is dotted with sculptures, most by Basque artists.

### Basílica de San Prudencio
Armentia s/n.

It's well worth the half-hour walk or the bus ride to see this church in the village of **Armentia**, now subsumed into Vitoria's outskirts. The village is supposedly the birthplace of San Prudencio, the patron saint of Alava, and the church was erected in his honour. Rebuilt in the 18th century, it still has some excellent features from its Romanesque youth, such as a harmonious round apse and the carvings above the doors, one of Christ and the apostles, the other of the Lamb and John the Baptist. To reach Armentia on foot, continue past the Museo de Bellas Artes on Paseo Fray Francisco de Vitoria, turn left down Paseo de Cervantes when you reach the La Sagrada Familia chapel. The basilica is at the end of this road.

## Casco Medieval

*Vitoria's shield-shaped old town sits on the high ground that perhaps gave the city its name; beturia is an Euskara word for hill. The town was founded and fortified by the kings of Navarra in the 12th and 13th centuries but was an obscure Castilian town for much of history. The Casco Medieval isn't a social hub like the old towns of Bilbao or San Sebastián's old towns but it's got a finer selection of architecture tucked inside some well preserved sections of wall. Some of the area seems a little run down, but not **Calle Cuchillería**, the axis, which is a street of studenty Basque bars. There are also a number of museums thoughtfully making use of some of the Casco's prettiest buildings.*

### Calle Cuchillería

This street, and its continuation, Calle Chiquita, is the most happening part of the old town, with several impressive old mansions, a couple of museums, dozens of bars, and plenty of pro-Basque political attitude. On weekend evenings the street is packed as every bar earns their bread keeping the entire student population in drink. Like several in the Casco Medieval, this street is named after the craftspeople that used to have shops here; in this case, makers of knives. At number 24 stands the impressive facade of the **Casa de Cordón**, a 15th-century building with an impressive carved cord of St Francis over the door. It houses occasional exhibitions. Walking along this street and those nearby you can see a number of old inscriptions and coats of arms carved on buildings.

## Iglesia de San Miguel
Plaza de la Virgen Blanca s/n.

This church stands side on to and above the Plaza de la Virgen Blanca like one of a series of chess pieces guarding the entrance to the Casco Medieval. Two gaping arches mark the portal, which is superbly carved. A niche here holds the city's patron saint, the Virgen Blanca, a late Gothic figure. On the saint's day, August 5, a group of townspeople carry the figure of *Celedón* (a stylised farmer) from the top of the graceful belltower down to the square.

## Los Arquillos
This strange series of dwellings and colonnades were designed in the early 19th century as a means of more effectively linking the high Casco Medieval with the newer town below, and to avoid the risk of the collapse of the southern part of the hill. It leads up to the attractive small **Plaza del Machete**, where incoming city chancellors used to swear an oath of allegiance over a copy of the *Fueros* (city statutes) and a machete, in this case a military cutlass.

## Plaza de España
The postcardy Plaza de España (the Basques call it Plaza Nueva) was designed by Olaguíbel, who thought up the Arquillos. It's a beautiful colonnaded square housing the town hall and several bars with terraces that are perfect for the morning or afternoon sun.
● *On C Cuchillería 54, housed in a beautiful fortified medieval house, the Museo Fournier de Naipes, T 945-181920, is an unusual museum devoted to the playing card.*

## Plaza de la Virgen Blanca

The pretty, open Plaza de la Virgen Blanca is centred around a memorial, commemorating the Battle of Vitoria on Midsummer's Day in 1813. Napoleon's forces were routed by the Allied troops and fled in ragged fashion towards home, abandoning their baggage train, containing millions of francs, which was gleefully looted. "The battle was to the French," commented a British officer sagely, "like salt on a leech's tail." The square is the town's social hub of the town, with many cafés around it.

## Palacio de Escoriaza-Esquibel
C de Fray Zacarías Martínez s/n.

This palace features one of the town's most seductive medieval façades. Built in 1540, it is plateresque – an ornate style of Spain's golden age that originally drew elements from the Moors and the Venetians before confidently coming into its own. Next to the palace, parts of the town's 12th-century walls are very well preserved.

## Catedral de Santa María
Plaza de Santa María s/n. *Tours: 1100, 1400, 1700, and 2000, check with the tourist office, or www.catedralvitoria.com for the current situation.* €2

Her Gothic Majesty the Cathedral of Santa María is undergoing a long-term renovation until 2009. While this is taking place, the massive 14th-century structure is closed to passing visitors. However, guided tours of the renovation works are being run when the state of play allows. The tours are interesting: the project is a massive one and involves considerable ingenuity and expertise.

We arrived at Bilbao
After two years and seven months I return to you,
cursed city and city locked deep in my heart…
City ever closer, ever harsher, ever rustier, ever
more cherished.
Bilbao.

*Blas de Otero*

**Museo de Arqueología**

C Correría 116, **T** 945-181922, **F** 945-181923.   *Tue-Fri 1000-1400, 1600-1830, Sat 1000-1400, Sun 1100-1400. Free.*

This corner of the old town is one of Vitoria's most picturesque. The **Casa del Portalón**, now a noted restaurant, is a lovely late 15th- century timbered building, once an inn and a staging post for messengers. Across from it is the **Torre de los Anda**, which defended one of the entrances in the city wall. Opposite is the 16th-century house of the Gobeo family now holds the archaeology museum. The small collection covers the prehistoric through Roman and mediaeval periods. Of the three floors of objects, arguably the most impressive is the so-called *Knight's Stele*, a tombstone carved with a horseman dating from the Roman era. The top floor contains panels on archaeology.

# Alava/Araba

The province of Alava is something of a wilderness compared to the densely settled valleys of Vizcaya and Guipúzcoa. The walled town of **Salvatierra** is a good base for exploring the area, while in the west the **Cañon de Delika** is a valley of considerable beauty, and the Salinas de Añana are an unusual sight, to say the least. North of Vitoria, the two large embalses are the place to go to hit the water in this landlocked zone, while the peak of **Gorbeia** is a spectacular climb. If you venture off the main roads you'll feel like an explorer in Alava; the tourist count is low here, even in high summer.

▸▸ *See Sleeping  p144, Eating and drinking p173*

## Western Alava

*West of Vitoria the green pastures soon give way to a rugged and dry terrain, home of vultures, eagles and spectacular rock formations. The area is fairly well served by bus from Vitoria.*

### Salinas de Añana
*Five buses daily from Vitoria bus station.*

This hard-bitten half-a-horse village has one of the more unusual sights in the Basque lands. The place owes its existence to the saline water that wells up from the ground, which was diverted down a valley and siphoned into any number of 'eras', flat evaporation platforms mounted on wooded stilts. It's an eerie sight, looking like the ruins of an ancient Greek city in miniature. As many as 5500 pans were still being used by the 1960s but nowadays there are only about 150. The first written reference to the salt collection in these parts was in 822AD, but it seems pretty likely the Romans had a go too.

There's an attractive church but not much else in the village, which has suffered badly since the decline of the salt pans. During Semana Santa, however, the place is more lively; Judas is put on trial by the villagers. It's something of a kangaroo court though; the poor man is always convicted and then burned.

### Cañon de Delika
*Access from a car park, about 3 km from the main road, the 2625 (running from Orduña in the north to Espejo in the south and beyond), turn-off is signposted Monte Santiago and is about 8 km south of Orduña). Buses to Orduña from Vitoria bus station with La Unión.*

To the west beyond Salinas, and actually reached via the province of Burgos, this spectacular canyon widens into the valley of Orduña. The River Nervión has its source near here, but it's sometimes hard to believe that this is the same river that made Bilbao great - it's regularly dry in summer. When running, it spectacularly spills 300 metres into the gorge below creating the highest waterfall in Spain. There's a good one and a half-hour round walk from the carpark. Follow the right-hand road first, which brings you to the falls, then follow the cliffs to the left, where vultures soar above the valley below. When you reach the second mirador, looking down to Orduña, another road descends through beech forest back to the car park. Near here is a spring, the **Fuente de Santiago**. Legend has it that St James stopped here to refresh himself and his horse during his alleged time in Spain.

● *If you're in a car, there's another waterfall to visit on the way back to Vitoria from Orduña. A marked side road near the town of Gujuli leads to it, prettily set beside a Romanesque church.*

# Eastern Alava

*The eastern half of the Alava plain is dotted with interesting villages, churches and prehistoric remains. The town of **Salvatierra** is the most convenient base for exploration. At the northern fringes of the plain, the mountains rise into Guipúzcoa. Part of the **Camino de Santiago** passes through the natural tunnel of San Adrián here, and there's some scenic walking to be done.*

---

### Salvatierra/Agurain
*3 trains daily from Vitoria (destination Pamplona), 15mins, €2.10.*

The major town in eastern Alava is the not-very-major Salvatierra (Agurain), a well-preserved walled mediaeval town with some interesting buildings. The sleeping and eating possibilities are nothing to write home about, but there are a couple of pensiones.

The tourist office, next to the **Iglesia de San Juan**, is very helpful. They currently hold keys for the churches in Salvatierra as well as the church at Gaceo (see below). Unfortunately, though, they don't have permission to lend the keys to visitors so currently the only option is to pay for a guided tour, €36, for either Gaceo or Salvatierra, so it's better if you can rustle up a posse to share the cost. Ring the tourist office to see if any tours have been booked, and you might be able to tag along.

### San Martín, Gaceo and La Asunción, Alaiza

*Gaceo: 5 buses daily to/from Vitoria/Salvatierra (destination Araia), falling to two Saturday and one Sunday. Alaiza: Bus from Salvatierra*

Although current arrangements make access problematic (see Salvatierra), the frescoes in this small village church are extremely impressive. The 13th-century building's interior is completely covered with the works, dated to the 14th century. They were rediscovered in the 1960s, having been hidden under a healthy coat of plaster. The major scene is a Trinity above the altar, a Crucifixion, and the Last Judgement, with St Michael carefully weighing souls.

Near by, in the village of Alaiza, the **Iglesia de La Asunción** is similarly painted, but in a bizarrely different, seemingly irreligious style and a childlike technique. It's far from high medieval art, but the pictures are extremely funny – to fans of toilet humour. The keyholder lives at number 26 on the right of the church.

### Túnel de San Adrián and around

*Five buses daily to Zalduondo from Vitoria/Salvatierra (destination Araia), falling to two Saturday and one Sunday.*

There's much walking to be done, as well as numerous adventure tourism options (see p 27). One of the most interesting walks starts from the hamlet of **Zalduondo**, 8 km north of Salvatierra. A section of one of the branches of the **Camino de Santiago**, part of it follows the old Roman/mediaeval highway that effectively linked most of the peninsula with the rest of Europe. It's about 5.5 km from Zalduondo to a small parking area named Zumarraundi. From there, the track ascends through beech forest to the Túnel de San Adrián. Shortly after the old stone road, there's a right turn up a slope, easily missed: look for the wooden signpost at the top of the rise to your right. The tunnel itself is a spectacular natural cave. It now houses a small chapel, perhaps built to assuage the fears of medieval pilgrims, who thought that the cave was the entrance to Hell. Another anecdote, related with glee by Basques, tells of a Castilian king who travelled eastwards to enforce his rights over Navarra boasting that he'd never in his life bowed his head or dismounted before any man, least of all Basques. On reaching the tunnel, (with the Navarran deputation smirking on the other side), he wasn't left with much choice…

After the tunnel, the trail continues into Guipúzcoa, reaching the attractive town of **Zegama** about 90-minutes' walk further on.

The area around Zalduondo and Salvatierra is notable for its series of dolmens. Near the village of **Eguilaz**, three-quarters of an hour's walk from Salvatierra (just off the N1 to the east) is the dolmen of **Aitzkomendi**, rediscovered by a farmer in 1830. The eleven impressive stones tip the scales at around the ten-ton mark. It's thought the dolmen was an early Bronze Age funerary marker.

On the other side of Salvatierra near Arrizala is the similarly impressive **Sorginetxe**, dated to a similar period. The name means 'house of the witch'; in the Middle Ages, the area could well have been the forest home of somebody of that profession. To the east of here, near the village of **Ilarduia**, is the **Leze cave**, a huge crevice in the cliff face, 80-metres high, access tricky. It's great for canyoning, see tours, p27.

## Los Embalses

*Buses to Urrúnaga and Legutiano or Ullibarri-Gamboa from Vitoria bus station.*

Not far north of Vitoria, two large artificial lakes help compensate Alavans for the landlocked nature of their province. Brought into existence to supply Vitoria with water, they are both popular recreational retreats from the capital. The larger of the two, the Embalse de Urribarri, is more populated, and the place to go for watersports, centred around the pretty town of Ullibarri-Gamboa. Urrúnaga, to the west, is most easily accessed from the town of Legutiano and has many secluded spots popular with anglers.

*Architectural innovation in Euskadi has spread right down to the conservative plains of the Basque Rioja. Santiago Calatrava's fluid winery design echoes the mountains in the background at the Ysios bodega.*

### Gorbeia
*Buses to Murguia from Vitoria bus station.*

Straddling Vizcaya and Alava is the massif of Gorbeia, an enticingly inaccessible area of peaks and gorges topped by the peak of the same name, which hits 1482 m when it remembers not to slouch. It features in Basque consciousness as a realm of deities and purity. There are several good marked trails around Murguia, including an ascent of the peak itself which shouldn't be attempted in poor weather.

## La Rioja Alavesa

*Basque Rioja? What's this? The two words don't seem to go together but in fact many of the finest Riojas are from Alava province. Confusion reigns because the Spanish province of La Rioja is only one of three that the wine region encompasses. Although it's not far from Vitoria, the Rioja Alavesa definitely feels Spanish rather than Basque; the descent from the green hills into the arid plains crosses a cultural border as well as a geographic one. The area offers the opportunity to visit some excellent vineyards, and the hilltop town of **Laguardia** is one of the most atmospheric places in Euskadi. The majority of Rioja winemaking is now done outside the old towns in more modern* *wineries. The Rioja Alavesa has 200-odd bodegas. The tourist office will provide a list. All require a phone call in advance to organise a visit; the more of you there are, the more willing most will be.*

---

## ★ Laguardia/Biasteri
*Buses from Vitoria bus station.*

---

The small walled hilltop town of Laguardia, standing at an altitude of 1500 feet, and with a population of 1500, commands the plain like a sentinel, which it was; it was originally called La Guardia de Navarra – the 'guard of Navarra'. Underneath the mediaeval streets, like catacombs, are over 300 small *bodegas*, cellars used for the making and storing of wine, and a place to hide in troubled times. Most are no longer used – **Bodega El Fabulista** (see below) is an exception.

The town itself is captivating. Founded in 1164, its narrow streets are lovely to wander. The impressive **Iglesia de Santa María de los Reyes**, begun in the 12th century, has a finely preserved painted Gothic façade (weekend tours; 1730 and 1830, €2, at other times keys available at the tourist office), while the former Ayuntamiento on Plaza Nueva was inaugurated in the 16th century.

Laguardia was the birthplace of the writer of fables Felix de Samaniego. His family was the richest in town, and their large residence is now divided between the tourist office and Bodega El Fabulista. The surrounding area also has a few non-vinous attractions. A set of small lakes close by is one of Spain's better spots for birdwatching, particularly from September to March when migrating species abound. There are a series of marked walking and cycling routes, spectacularly backed by the **Sierra Cantábrica**. If you're coming from Vitoria by car, it's marginally quicker and more scenic to take the A2124 rather than the motorway. After ascending to a pass, the high ground dramatically drops away to the Riojan plain; there's a superb lookout, *El Balcón* (the balcony).

## Dolmen sites
*La Hoya open Oct-Apr Tue-Sat 1100-1500, Sun 1000-1400; May-Sep Tue-Fri 1100-1400, 1600-2000, Sat 1100-1500, Sun 1000-1400. Free*

Extensively settled in prehistoric times, the area has numerous dolmens, some within walking distance of the town. The best, Hechicera, is 6 km to the east, near the town of Elvillar. It dates to about 2100BC. About a 1,000 years later the Iron Age settlement of La Hoya was founded. There's a small museum at the site, which is just north of Laguardia and worth a look.

## Bodegas Palacio
Ctra de Elciego s/n, **T** 945-600057/5621195, www.cosmepalacio. com   *Tours : Tue-Sun at 1230 and 1330, €3 (redeemable in shop or restaurant). Booking essential. Easy walking distance from Laguardia.*

One of the handiest of the wineries, and worth seeing, Bodegas Palacio, is just below Laguardia on the Elciego road, some 10-minute's walk from town. The winery is modern; the older *bodega* alongside has been charmingly converted into a hotel and restaurant. Palacio produces a range of wines, the quality of which has improved over recent years. Their *Glorioso* and *Cosme Palacio* labels are widely sold in the UK. Having until recently been owned by the Canadian multinational *Seagrams*, Palacio is well geared to visitors, and runs daily tours (which must be booked by phone). The informative tours are  in Spanish, but English guides are available.

The winery was originally founded in 1894 and is fairly typical of the area, producing 90% red wine from the Tempranillo grape, and 10% of white from Viura. The altitude in these parts means that the grapes ripen slowly, and the vintage is in the first week of October, comparatively late for Spain. As well as *crianzas*, *reservas*, and *gran reservas* (see box, page 116), Palacio also produce a red wine for drinking young, which is soft, fruity, and a change from the heavier

## ▶ Wine

In good Catholic fashion, wine is the blood of Spain. It's the standard accompaniment to most meals, but also features very prominently in bars, where a glass of cheap *tinto* or *blanco* can cost as little as €0.30, although it's normally more. The two principal wine denominations in the Basque lands are *txakolí*, produced near the coast between Bilbao and San Sebastián; and Rioja, one of whose three regions lies in Alava south of Vitoria.

*Txakolí* (chacolí) has a small production which was awarded DO (*Denominación de Origen*, similar to the French *appelation controlée*) status in 1990. The most common form is a young, refreshing, acidic white which has a green tinge and a slight sparkle, often accentuated by pouring from a height. The best examples, from around Getaria, go beautifully with seafood. Made from underripe grapes of the Ondarrubi Zuria variety; there's a less common red and rosé variety.

The overall standard of Riojas has improved markedly since the granting of the higher DOC status in 1991, involving stringent testing. The Basque section, the Rioja Alavesa, produces many of the region's best wines, which are mostly fullish-bodied reds from the Tempranillo grape (with three other permitted red grapes often used to add depth or character). Whites from Viura and Malvasia are also produced: the majority of these are young, fresh, and dry, unlike the powerful oaky Rioja whites sold in the UK. Rosés are also produced. The quality of individual Riojas varies widely according to both producer and the amount of time the wines have been aged in oak barrels and in the bottle. The words crianza, reserva, and gran reserva refer to the length of the aging process, while the vintage date is also given. Among other regions, neighbouring Navarra is producing some quality wines unfettered by the stricter rules governing Rioja production. The Ribera del Duero region, meanwhile, has been building a reputation for red wines of the highest quality. It's been dubbed "the Spanish Burgundy", and the description isn't altogether misplaced; the better wines have the rich nose and delicate earthy quality of the better reds from that area. Rueda, around Valladolid, produces some excellent dry whites from the Verdejo and Viura grapes. In many bars, you can order Ribera, Rueda or other regions by the glass. If you ask for crianza or reserva, you'll get a Rioja.

*Crianza*: A red crianza must be at least two years old, six months of which have been spent in oak (twelve in the case of Rioja).

*Reserva*: A red reserva has passed its third birthday, of which twelve months (often more) have been in oak

*Gran Reserva*: The softest and most charracterful of the Riojas, although sometimes tends to be overaged. At least five years old, with two or more in oak. Only produced in good years

*Cosechero*: A young red usually produced by carbonic maceration, where the whole grapes begin to ferment in carbon dioxide before being pressed. This gives a fruity, slightly fizzy wine – a good match for many of the region's hearty foods.

*Vino Corriente/Normal/de Mesa*: The cheap option in bars and restaurants, table wine which can vary from terrible to reasonable. Often high in acid, which balances the oily Spanish food. Served in a tumbler in bars so there's no pretending.

*Fresco*: Most bars will keep a bottle of red fresco, or chilled; a refreshing hot weather option

*Kalimotxo*: The drink of choice for students, red wine mixed 50-50 with Coca-Cola. Often served in *katxis*, paper cups holding a litre that are nursed solo or shared with straws.

*Vino Generoso*: Generous, ie fortified, wine, such as sherry.

Rioja styles. The tour improves after the introductory video, and you get the chance to taste a couple of the wines. Palacio run monthly tasting weekends; two nights in the hotel, a tasting session and some meals, for €300 for two people.

## Bodega El Fabulista
Plaza San Juan s/n, Laguardia, **T** 945-621192.  *Tours daily at 1130, 1300, and 1730, €4.81.*

A massive contrast to Palacio, which produces two-million bottles a year, is Bodega El Fabulista, next to the tourist office in Laguardia. The owner Eusebio, effectively runs the place alone and produces about one-fiftieth of that amount. The wine is made using very traditional methods in the intriguing underground cellar from grapes he grows himself. He runs three tours a day, which are excellent, and include lots of background information on the Rioja wine region and a generous tasting in a beautiful underground vault. The wines, marketed as *Decidido*, are good young-drinking reds and whites. The tours are in Spanish, but English and French guides can be arranged with advance notice, but it's still worth doing the tour just to have a look and a taste!

## Herederos del Marqués de Riscal
C Torrea 1, Elciego, **T** 945-606000 (Mon-Fri), www.marquesderiscal .com  *Some of the buses running between Vitoria and Logroño stop in Elciego and Laguardia, 7 km away.*

Founded in 1860, Marqués de Riscal is the oldest and best known of the Rioja *bodegas* and has built a formidable reputation for the quality of its wines. The Marqués himself was a Madrid journalist who, having cooled off in France after getting in some hot political water at home, started making wine on his return to Spain. Enlisting the help of Monsieur Pinot, a French expert, he experimented by planting Cabernet Sauvignon, which is still used today.

The winery is modern but remains faithful to the *bodega*'s rigorous tradition of quality. The historic collection of Riscal wines includes some bottles from as far back as 1862. As well as the traditionally elegant *Reserva* and *Gran Reserva*, the more recently inaugurated *Baron de Chirel* is a very classy red indeed, coming from low-yielding old vines and exhibiting more French character than is typical of the region.

The innovative spirit continues, and Marqués de Riscal has enlisted none other than Frank Gehry of Guggenheim Museum fame to design its new visitors' complex, which will include a hotel, restaurant, and exhibition centre, as well as other facilities. Due to open in late 2004, the building will be another visual treat; Gehry's design (a model of which is visible at the *bodega*) incorporates ribbons of coloured titanium over a building of natural stone. The silver, gold, and 'dusty rose' sheets are Gehry's response to "the unbroken landscape of vineyards and rich tones".

For the moment the *bodega* welcomes interested visitors by prior appointment only, and it's usually essential to reserve several weeks in advance.

Elciego is a pleasant little village with a hotel and the chunkily beautiful church of **San Andrés**, with its one massive arched nave.

## Other wineries

North of Laguardia, with a waved design echoing the steep mountains, is the **Ysios** bodega, designed by Santiago Calatrava, the Valencian engineer/architect who has made the Basque Country his second home. Twenty minutes east of Laguardia is the pretty but parched town of **Oyon/Oion**. One of the bigger operations here is Bodegas Faustino Martínez (T 945-622500), not as geared to visitors as might be expected, but they run a good in-depth tour in Spanish or English – but it's thirsty work with no tasting at the end. Oyon has an excellent restaurant, **El Mesón La Cueva.**

**Museums and galleries**

**Bilbao**
- **Guggenheim Museum** The epitomy of Bilbao's transformation, p40.
- **Museo Arqueológico, Etnológico y Histórico Vasco** Basque artifacts covering thousands of years, p35.
- **Museo de Bellas Artes de Bilbao** An excellent collection of mostly Spanish art, p47.
- **Museo Diocesano de Arte Sacro** Good collection of religious art set around a lovely cloister, p36.

**San Sebastián**
- **Kutxaespacio de la Ciencia** Interactive science museum, p94.
- **Museo Chillida-Leku** A great number of works by the late Basque sculptor Eduardo Chillida, p94.
- **Museo de San Telmo** A wide-ranging collection of pieces, including much Basque art both modern and older, p89.
- **Museo Naval** A dryish museum on Basque naval heritage, p86.

**Vitoria**
- **Artium** An exciting building devoted to modern Basque art, p99.
- **Museo de Arqueología** Pieces through the ages, p107.
- **Museo de Bellas Artes** A collection of Basque art, p101.

**The Basque Country**
- **Museo Gernika** Documents about the Civil War, p63.
- **Museo Ignacio Zuloaga, Zumaia** Works by Zuloaga, p97.
- **Museo de Simón Bolívar**, Bolibar (near Markina), p67.
- **Museo Zumalacárregui**, Ormaiztegi The childhood home of Tomás Zumalacárregui, swashbuckling general, p69.

The standard of accommodation in the Basque country is very high: even the most modest of *pensiones* are usually very clean and respectable. Places to stay (*alojamientos*) are divided into three main categories; *Hoteles* (marked H or HR) are graded from one to five stars, which distinguishes them from *hostales* (Hs or HsR), which go from one to three stars. *Pensiones* (P) are the standard budget option, and are usually family-run flats in an apartment block. An excellent option if you've got transport is the network of *agroturismos* and *casas rurales*. The best of these are traditional Basque farmhouses. Many are in picturesque settings, and most offer exceptional value. While some are listed in this section, the tourist offices in the region will provide you with a booklet listing all of them. There are a few official youth hostels in the Basque region, but the price of *pensiones* rarely makes it worth the trouble except for solo travellers. Spanish youth hostels frequently are populated by noisy schoolkids, and have curfews and check-out times unsuitable for the late hours the locals keep.

€ **Sleeping codes**

**Price**

| | | | |
|---|---|---|---|
| LL | €150 and over | C | €45-60 |
| L | €120-150 | D | €38-45 |
| AL | €100-120 | E | €30-38 |
| A | €80-100 | F | €20-30 |
| B | €60-80 | G | €20 and under |

Prices refer to the cost of a double room in high season including taxes

Most campsites in the Basque country are on the coast, and are set up as well-equipped holiday villages for holidaying families. In other areas, camping, unless specifically prohibited, is a matter of common sense: most locals will know of (or offer) a place where you can pitch a tent *tranquilamente*. All registered accommodations charge a 7% value-added tax; this is often included at cheaper places and may be waived if you pay cash (tut tut).

# Bilbao/Bilbo

## Casco Viejo

**L** (**A** at weekends) **Hotel Tryp Arenal**, C Fueros 2, **T** 944-153100, **F** 944-156395, tryp.arenal@solmelia.com *Map 1, C2, p 247* In a colourful building on the edge of Casco Viejo, this is a comfortable chain hotel with well-appointed doubles and slightly cramped singles. Spick and span, and significantly cheaper weekend rates.

**A Barceló Hotel Avenida**, Avda Zumalacárregui 40, 48006, **T** 94 4-12 4300, **F** 944-11 46 17, www.bchotels.com/avenida *Map 2, A6, p249* Five minutes from Casco Viejo, this business-oriented hotel has 143 rooms and great panoramic views of the city.

**Arriaga**, C Ribera 3, **T** 944-790001, **F** 944-790516. *Map 1,*
Very friendly hotel with a garage and some excellent
ith floor-to-ceiling windows and views over the theatre.
Plush, formal-style decoration and fittings. Good value. Parking
underneath for €10.80 per night.

**B Hotel Sirimiri**, Plaza de la Encarnación 3, **T** 944-330759,
**F** 944-330875. www.hotelsirimiri.com  hsirimiri@euskalnet.net
*Map 1, F6, p247*  Named after the light misty rain that is a feature of
the city, this is a gem of a hotel in a quiet square. The genial owner
has equipped it with a gym and sauna, and there is free parking.
Rooms come with TV, air-con, and phone.

**C/E Hostal Mendéz**, C Santa María 13, **T** 944-160364.  *Map 1, E2,*
*p247*  Dignified building with castle-sized doors and an entrance
guarded by iron dogs. The first floor has *hostal*-grade rooms with
new bathrooms. The fourth floor is pensión-style, simpler, but
adequate, many rooms with balconies.

**C  Iturrienea Ostatua**, C Santa María, **T** 944-161500, **F** 944-
158929.  *Map 1, E2, p 247*  This beautiful pensión is caringly lined in
stone, wood, and ideosyncratic objects. With delicious breakfasts
and homely rooms, you might want to move in.

**D Hostal La Estrella**, C María Muñoz 6, **T** 944-164066. *Map 1, D4,*
*p247*  A reasonable if overpriced Casco Viejo option that has seen
slightly better days, but has spacious rooms with or without bathroom, all-night access, and a bar. The rooms with balcony are nice,
but can be noisy in the mornings.

**E Hostal Gurea**, C Bidebarrieta 14, **T** 944-163299. *Map 1, E2,*
*p247*  Carefully refurbished and well-scrubbed establishment on
one of Casco Viejo´s principal axes. Welcoming and cheerfully
vague about bookings. Usually request a 0100 curfew.

Sleeping

**E Hostal Mardones**, C Jardines 4, **T** 944-153105. *Map 1, E2, p247* Run by a welcoming and chatty owner and very well situated in *pintxo* heartland. Entered by the side of a newsstand, the pensión is fitted in attractive dark wood, and both exterior and interior rooms are pleasant, light and airy.

**E Hostal Roquefe**r, C Lotería 2, **T** 944-150755. *Map 1, E3 p247* A last resort but usually the last place to fill up. Some of the rooms are quite pleasant, but others are shabby and stuffy. Overpriced.

**F Pensión Ladero**, C Lotería 1, **T** 944-150932. *Map 1, E3, p247* Across the road from the Roquefer, this welcoming option has cork tiles, good shared bathrooms, and well-priced rooms, with TV, some of which are reached by a tiny spiral staircase. Can be noisy in the mornings.

**F Pensión Manoli**, C Libertad 2, **T** 944-155636. *Map 1 C3, p247* In the heart of the Casco Viejo, with some good-value exterior rooms with balcony and shared bathroom. Bright and well looked after.

### Riverbank

**L Gran Domine**, Alameda Mazarredo 61, **T** 944-211198. **F** 944-253301. www.hoteles-silken.com/dominebil.htm *Metro: Moyúa. Map 2, C6, p248* Opened summer 2002, this five-star hotel is directly opposite the Guggenheim and has been designed by innovative Basque architect Iñaki Aurrekoetxea. The distinctive façade of the building consists of forty-eight mirrors at slightly different angles, while the interior is dominated by a large central atrium. Service is of a high order and, like its sister hotel the Indautxu, the Domaine has bags more character than most top-end establishments.

**L Hotel Nervión**, C Paseo Campo Volantín 11, **T** 944-454700, **F** 944-455608. *Metro: Casco Viejo.* *Map 2, A10, p249*
The cavernous lobby of this modish luxury hotel includes a piano which is the focus of a weekly jazz session. The well-designed rooms offer all the expected comforts, including the business traveller´s delight, Playstation. Some rooms have good river views.

**AL Hotel Conde Duque**, Paseo Campo Volantín 22, **T** 944-456000, **F** 944-456066. *Metro: Casco Viejo.* *Map 2, A9, p249* An agreeable riverfront hotel, and fairly thoughtfully decorated despite a slightly tired façade. The rooms, complete with safe, phone and minibar, offer decent comfort. Midway between the Guggenheim and the Casco Viejo. Restaurant has a €10.20 menú at lunch and dinner.

**C Hostal Begoña**, C Amistad 2, **T** 944-230134, **F** 944-230133. *Metro: Abando.* *Map 2, C12, p249* A recent refit has transformed the Begoña into a welcoming modern hotel, with flair and comfort. From the inviting library/lounge to the large chalet-style rooms and mini-suites at very reasonable prices, this is an excellent option. The hotel offers free internet, and organizes a range of out-door activities.

**C Pensión Bilbao**, C Amistad 2, **T** 944-246943, **F** 944-352426. *Metro: Abando.* *Map 2, C12, p249* Neat rooms with bath in a refur-bished building just across the river from Casco Viejo. While a little small, the exterior ones have balconies with geraniums in window boxes.

## El Ensanche

**LL Hotel Carlton**, Plaza Moyúa 2, **T** 944-162200, **F** 944-164628, *Metro: Moyúa.* *Map 2, E8, p249* This grand old hotel, set on noisy Plaza Moyúa, is considerably more luxurious inside than out. Its

★ **Pensiones with a bit of charm**

Best

- •Iturrienea Ostatua, Casco Viejo, Bilbao, p124.
- •Ladero, Casco Viejo, Bilbao, p125.
- •Gran Bahía, Parte Vieja, San Sebastián, p137.
- •Amaiur, Parte Vieja, San Sebastián, p137.
- •Hostal Itxas-Gain, Getaria ,p142.

refurbished neo-classical ambience has colonnaded Einstein, Lorca, and Hemingway among other notables.

**LL Hotel Ercilla**, C Ercilla 37-39, **T** 944-705700, **F** 944-439335, www.hotelercilla.es *Metro: Indautxu. Map 2, G7, p249* Well located on the city's main shopping street, this four-star hotel has a cheerful entrance and helpful service. It's undergoing a gradual renovation, and the rooms in the newer section are much the better for it. There are excellent weekend rates, with savings up to 40%. Check the website for current offers. The hotel restaurant, *Bermeo*, is excellent.

**LL Hotel Lopez de Haro**, C Obispo Orueta 2, **T** 944-235500, **F** 944-234500, lh@hotellopezdeharo.com *Metro: Moyúa. Map 2, C9, p249* A modern but characterful five-star hotel in classic style. While there are better value hotels, it's popular for its genuinely helpful service and excellent restaurant. Check the website for special deals.

**L Hotel Indautxu**, Plaza Bombero Etxariz s/n, **T** 944-211198, **F** 944-22133. *Metro: Indautxu. Map 2, H8, p249* Behind a mirrored façade which bizarrely dwarfs the older building in front are comfortable executive-style rooms, overlook a comparatively quiet square. There's a terrace, and pianists make the odd scheduled appearance in the bar. More character than many in this category and cheerful.

**L Hotel Jardines de Albia**, C San Vicente 6, **T** 944-354140, **F** 944-354142. *Metro: Abando. Map 2, C10, p249* Set in a peaceful back street near the gardens for which it is named, and fronted by a mermaid, this is another upmarket hotel that offers substantial weekend discounts. Fairly attractively furnished, and the rooms are more homely than might be expected. Spa and hydrotherapy centre in the building.

**A Hotel Hesperia Zubialde**, Camino de la Ventosa 34, **T** 944-008100, **F** 944-008110. *Metro: San Mamés. Map 2, H3, p248.* This is the nicest of the cluster of hotels catering to the trade fair hall and congress centre at this end of town. In a free-standing restored building away from the downtown bustle, it's modern and efficient but pleasant. There's a terrace café and a very reasonably priced restaurant. It's got sweeping views over the river, but the waterfront beautification definitely hasn't reached here yet.

**B Hotel Vista Alegre**, C Pablo Picasso 13, **T** 944-431450, **F** 944-431454. *Euskotren: Zabálburu. Map 2, H11, p249* A characterful if faded hotel near the bullring, with lots of old Basque prints, a certain stuffy plushness, and considerate staff.

**C Hostal Central**, Alameda Rekalde 35, **T** 944-106339, **F** 944-701576. *Metro: Moyúa. Map 2, F8, p248* True to its name, this newish option is right in the centre of the city, a block from Plaza Moyúa in prime shopping territory. The rooms are quite attractive, and there's a good feeling about the place; they seem more at home with tourists than business travellers. Internet access available.

**C Hotel Zabálburu**, C Pedro Martínez Artola 8, **T** 944-437100, **F** 944-100073. *Euskotren: Zabálburu. Map 2, H10, p249* Although not in the most attractive part of Bilbao, this hotel is attentive and comfortable. Parking is available for €8.

**Albergue Bilbao Aterpetxea**, Ctra Basurto-Kastrexana 70, **T** 944-270054, **F** 944-275479. Bus 58 from Plaza Circular and the bus station.    Bilbao's cheerful HI hostel is a block-of-flats-sized structure by a motorway on the outskirts of Bilbao. Despite its inconvenient location, it does have good facilities (including bike hire), although it may well be flooded with school groups. It's just about the cheapest bed in town for single travellers, but couples won't have much, and the 0930 check-out is a shock to the system. There's a dining room with full meal service, but no kitchen facilities. Around €12.50 per person depending on season.

## Deusto

A **Hotel Deusto**, C Francisco Maciá 9, **T** 944-760006, **F** 944-762199, *Metro: Deusto. Map 2, D2, p248*  This colourfully decorated hotel is an enjoyable place to stay on this side of the river. The large rooms, featuring minibar, safe, Playstation and inviting beds are complemented by an attractively arty bar and restaurant downstairs.

B **Hotel Artetxe**, Camino de Berriz 112, **T** 944-747780, **F** 944-746020.  High above Deusto on the Artxanda ridge, this renovated farmhouse offers superb views over the whole city. With attractive wooden furnishings and small but homely bedrooms with beams and views, it's a great place to stay; but not that handy to get into Bilbao without a car.

C **Hotel Plaza San Pedro**, C Luzarra 7, **T** 944-763126, **F** 944-763895. *Metro: Deusto. Map 2, D1, p248:*  Disconcertingly set on a back street of automobile workshops, this hotel is pretty close to the centre of Deusto life, attractively modern, and well priced.

## Getxo, Portugalete and Beaches

A **Gran Hotel Puente Colgante**, C María Díaz de Haro 2,
**T** 944-014800, **F** 944-014810. *Euskotren: Portugalete. Metro: Areeta.* Very recently opened in a reconstructed 19th-century building with a grand façade, this upmarket modern hotel is superbly situated right next to the Puente Vizcaya on the waterfront promenade. All the rooms face outwards, and the hotel has all the facilities you come to expect.

A **Hotel Igeretxe**, Playa de Ereaga s/n, **T** 944-910009,
**F** 944-608599. *Metro: Neguri.* Shaded by palms, this welcoming hotel is right on Ereaga beach, Getxo's main social strand. Formerly a balneario, the hotel still offers some spa facilities, as well as a restaurant overlooking the slightly grubby sand. Breakfast included.

A **Hotel Los Chopos**, Av Los Chopos 2, **T** 944-912255,
**F** 944-912802. *Metro: Neguri.* A stylish hotel with a garden, peaceful despite the busy road. Away from Getxo's main bustle, it's attractively, if formally, furnished with cheerfull, welcoming bedrooms.

A **Hotel Los Tamarises**, Muelle de Ereaga 2, **T** 944-910005,
**F** 944-911310. *Metro: Neguri.* Another beachfront option, not as pretty as the Igeretxe but with considerably plusher rooms and similarly good views. There's a huge café-restaurant ensemble with a terrace that's a prime Getxo meeting point in summer.

B **Hotel Neguri**, Algortako Etorbidea 14, **T** 944-910509.
*Metro: Neguri.* On the main road, this boutique hotel has seen sprucer days but is charming and is refreshingly un-businessy.

D **Pensión Usategi**, C Landene 2, **T** 944-913918. *Metro: Bidezabal.* Well placed on the headland above pretty Arrigunaga beach. The rooms are clean and cool, and some have great views.

**E Pensión Areeta**, C Mayor 13 (Las Arenas), **T** 944-638136.
*Metro: Areeta.* Near the metro of the same name and a iron bar's throw from the Puente Vizcaya, this is a good place in the heart of the trendy Las Arenas district of Getxo.

**Camping Arrien**, Bld Uresarantze s/n, **T** 94-6770878,
**F** 94-6774480. *Metro: Plentzia.* Although not as convenient for Bilbao as the Sopelana (below), this campsite, connected regularly by bus with the Plentzia metro stop, is handy for the beach and boasts all the facilities. The bungalows are reasonable value for four or more. Open all year.

**Camping Sopelana**, Ctra Bilbao-Plentzia s/n, **T** 94-6762120.
*Metro: Sopelana.* Very handy for the Metro into Bilbao, this is the most convenient campsite within range of the city. Well-equipped with facilities, and in easy range of the shops, it's right by the beach too. Reasonable value bungalows available.

## Inland

### Gernika

**B Hotel Gernika**, C Carlos Gangoiti 17, **T** 94-6254948,
**F** 94-6255874. Gernika's best hotel is nothing exceptional, with uninteresting rooms in an ugly brick building on the edge of town. There's a bar and café, and the service is helpful.

**B Hotel Katxi**, Morga/Andra Mari s/n, **T** 94-6270740,
**F** 94-6270245. A few kilometres west of Gernika in the hamlet of Morga is this excellent rural hotel. The rooms, some larger than others, are extremely comfortable, and there's a friendly lounge area. It's a great place to get away from things a little, in a warm atmosphere. The same owners run a good asador next door.

**D Hotel Boliña**, C Barrenkale 3, **T** 94-6250300, **F** 94-6250304.
In the centre of Gernika, this hotel has some good-value doubles
with TV and telephone. Can be stuffy in summer.

**E Bizketxe**, Oma 8, **T** 94-6254906, **F** 94-6255573. In the perfect
Basque hamlet of Oma, underneath the painted wood, this is an
excellent place to stay if you've got transport. Lovely rooms in a
traditional farmhouse, with or without bath.

**E Pensión Akelarre**, C Barrenkale 5, **T** 94-6270197, **F** 94-
6270675. Funky little rooms with TV and floorboards. There's a
sunny terrace and it's in the heart of the pedestrian area.

**E Pensión Madariaga**, C Industria 10, **T** 94-6256035.
Very attractively furnished little place with rooms with TV,
bathroom, and welcoming furniture, for not a great deal of cash.

**F Ugaldeberri**, **T/F** 94-6256577, elenaelan@euskalnet.net
Located on the eastern side of the estuary, with superb views over
the reserve, this big farmhouse has three doubles; an excellent place
to stay if you've got a motor. Guests can use the kitchen.

## Elorrio

**B Hotel Elorrio**, Bº San Agustín s/n, Elorrio, **T** 94-6231555,
**F** 94-6231663. A short walk from the centre on the Durango road,
this modern hotel is not the prettiest but has some good views
around the valley and a decent restaurant. As it's primary function
is for business, it's a fair bit cheaper come the weekend. The rooms
are attractive, airy, and light.

**G Pensión Nerea**, C Pio X 32, Elorrio. A budget-traveller's dream
with perfectly adequate rooms with shared bathrooms for a
pittance. If no-one's about, go to the *tintorería* at C Labakua 8.

There are three *agroturismos* in the countryside around Elorrio, all set in typically solid and attractive Basque farmhouses.

**D Berriolope**, in the hamlet of Berrio, **T** 94-6820640 is the most luxurious of the three with six attractive doubles with bathroom in a vine-covered stone building.

**E Arabio Azpikoa**, Barrio Arabio 8, **T** 94-6583342, has simpler but very pleasant rooms with shared bathrooms.

**F Galartxa Barrena**, Zenita, **T** 94-6582707, is the closest to Elorrio, and has rooms with or without bath.

## Markina

**E/D Hotel Vega**, C Abasua 2, Markina, **T** 94-6166015. This sleepy place on the square is a relaxing base and has rooms both with and without bathroom.

**Monte Baserria**, Barrio Arta 23, near Bolibar, **T** 944-130987/ 606255424. A big house not far from the tiny village of Bolibar that can be rented for a weekend or by the week. It can work out very cheap, **E**, for a large group. It's a good base for walking in the surrounding area and comfortably sleeps up to seven.

## Oñati and Arantzazu

The cheaper beds in Oñati tend to fill up quickly at weekends. There's a small unmarked *pensión* above Bar Paco at C Zaharra 4; it's also worth asking the owner of the sweet stall in the main square, who rents a couple of rooms out.

**C Ongi**, C Zaharra 19, Oñati, **T** 943-718285, **F** 943-718284. A family-run well-decorated hotel on the main pedestrian street.

**E Goiko Venta**, Arantzazu 12, **T** 943-781305, **F** 943-780321.
Up the hill with good rooms, some with a great view of the valley.

**E Hospedería de Arantzazu**, Arantzazu 29, **T** 943-781313,
**F** 943-781314.   Right next to the basilica, offering fairly simple
rooms in a slightly pious atmosphere.

**F Echeverria**, C Barria 15, Oñati, **T** 943-780460.   A cheap *pensión*
not far from the main square. Its clean rooms are good value but
it's definitely worth ringing ahead at weekends.

**E Arreg**, Ctra Garagaltza-Auzoa 21, **T** 943-780824.   An excellent
*agroturismo* a couple of kilometres from town. A big farmhouse in
a green valley with beautiful dark-wood rooms, a ping-pong table,
and good folk running it.

## The Basque Coastline

### Bermeo and Mundaka

**B Hotel Atalaya**, C Itxaropen 1, Mundaka, **T** 94-6177000, **F** 94-
6876899, www.hotel-atalaya-mundaka.com   The classier of the
town's options, with a summery feel to its rooms . Garden and
parking adjoin the stately building. Nice breakfasts.

**C Hotel Arimune**, C Bentalde 95, Bakio, **T** 94-6194022.   Right on
the beach, cheerily strewn with honeysuckle, and more originally
decorated than many a beach hotel. The terrace is a peaceful spot
out of peak season. Closed Dec-Feb.

**C Hotel El Puerto**, Portu Kalea 1, Mundaka, **T** 94-6876725,
**F** 94-6876726, hotelelpuerto@euskalnet.net   Perhaps the best
value of Mundaka's three hotels, this is set right by the tiny fishing

harbour and has cute rooms, some overlooking the harbour (worth paying the few extra euros for). The bar below is one of Mundaka's best.

C **Hostal Torre Ercilla**, C Talaranzko 14, Bermeo, **T** 94-6187598, **F** 94-6884231, fbarrotabernav@nexo.es   A lovely place to stay in Bermeo's old town, between museum and church. The rooms are thoughtfully designed for relaxation, with small balconies, reading nooks, and soft carpet. There's also a lounge, terrace, chessboard and barbecue, among other comforts.

D **Hostal Aldatzeta**, C Erremedio 24, Bermeo, **T** 94-6187703. Small and attractive hotel not far from the port with soberly pretty exterior rooms with bathroom and TV.

**Camping Portuondo**, 1 km out of Mundaka on the road to Gernika, **T/F** 94-6877701, www.campingportuondo.com Sardined during the summer months, this is a well-equipped campsite with a swimming pool, café and laundry. The bungalows, with kitchen, fridge and television, sleep up to four, but are not significantly cheaper than the hotels in town.

## Lekeitio and around

C **Emperatriz Zita**, Santa Elena Etorbidea s/n, Lekeitio, **T** 94-6842655, **F** 94-6243500, www.saviat.net  This slightly odd-looking hotel was built on the site of a palace where Empress Zita lived in the 1920s. Married to the last Austro-Hungarian emperor, who unluckily acceded to the throne in a losing position in WW1, she was left with 8 children when he died of pneumonia on Madeira in 1922. The hotel is furnished in appropriately elegant style and is also a thalassotherapy (seawater) and health centre. The rooms are very pleasant and well-priced for the location and quality, as is the restaurant.

**C Hotel Zubieta**, Portal de Atea, Lekeitio, **T** 94-6843030, **F** 94-6841099, www.hotelzubieta.com  A superbly converted coachhouse in the grounds of a *palacio*. Considering its surprisingly low prices, this is one of the best places to stay in Euskal Herría, with friendly management, a lively bar, and cosy rooms with sloping wooden ceilings. Definitely one to pre-book at weekends. Highly recommended. The hotel also has reasonably priced two- and four-berth apartments attached to the hotel in Lekeitio.

**D/C Piñupe Hotela**, Av Pascual Abaroa 10, Lekeitio, **T** 94-6842984, **F** 94-6840772. The cheapest place in town, and a sound choice. The rooms are ensuite with phone and TV, and are plenty more comfortable than the bar downstairs would indicate.

**E-C Arrigorri**, Arrigorri 3, Ondarroa, **T** 94-6134045, **F** 94-6833307.  A good option across the river from the centre of Ondarroa, right on the beach. There are a variety of rooms with differing prices; the best have sea views. Friendly and comfortable. Breakfast included.

**F Patxi**, Arta Bide 21, Ondarroa, **T** 60-9986446.  One of only two options in Ondarroa, this is an exceedingly low-priced *pensión* that has colourful and comfortable rooms with a basic shared bathroom.

# San Sebastián/Donostia

### Parte Vieja

**B Hotel Parma**, C General Jauregui 11, Parte Vieja, **T** 943-428893, **F** 943-424082, www.hotelparma.com  *Map 4, A5, p252*  A fairly bland modern hotel whose happiest features are its location by the rivermouth and good views of the Kursaal from the better rooms.

**C/B Pensión Gran Bahía**, C Embeltrán 16, Parte Vieja, **T** 943-420216, www.paisvasco.com/granbahia *Map 4, B4, p252* Very attractive luxury *pensión* convenient for both the beach and Parte Vieja. The comfy beds sport leopard-print covers and the rooms are extremely quiet. Immaculately maintained, the place is run in Belle-Époque style. Non-smoking.

**C Pensión Itxasoa**, C San Juan 14, Parte Vieja, **T/F** 943-420132, itxasoa@pensionesconencanto.com *Map 4, A4, p252* This well located and attractively decorated pensión has great views over the rivermouth and out to sea. Helpful and welcoming.

**D/E Pensión Anne**, C Esterlines 15, Parte Vieja, **T** 943-421438, pensionanne@euskalnet.net *Map 4, B4, p252* Behind an imposing wooden door is a spotlessly new pensión. All rooms are exterior, with heating, TV, and optional bathroom.

**D Pensión Boulevard**, Alameda del Boulevard 24, Parte Vieja, **T** 943-429405. *Map 4, B4, p252* The San Lorenzo's sister set-up, with similar facilities, although not quite as homely. All rooms have bathroom, TV and fridge, and it's run with a smile.

**E Pensión Amaiur**, C 31 de Agosto 44, Parte Vieja, **T** 943-429654, amaiur@telefonica.net *Map 4, B3, p252* Situated in the oldest surviving house in the Parte Vieja (few others survived the 1813 fire), this is one of the best budget options in town. Lovingly decorated and sympathetically run, there are a variety of smallish but homely rooms, most with satellite TV, some with balconies. Guests have free use of the pretty (stoveless) kitchen, and there's high-speed Internet.

**E Pensión Larrea**, C Narrica 21, Parte Vieja, **T** 943-422694. *Map 4, B4, p252* A well-situated pensión with cheerful management, the rooms are all exterior with small balconies, and the shared bathrooms are clean. Prices are often negotiable.

**F Pensión Aussie**, C San Jerónimo 23, Parte Vieja, **T** 943-422874.
*Map 4, B3, p252*  Favourite of backpackers, particularly from south
of the equator. Rooms vary, and are run on the hostel principle by
the solicitous, if unpredictable, boss, inevitably nicknamed Skippy.

**F-D Pensión San Lorenzo**, C San Lorenzo 2, Parte Vieja,
**T** 943-425516, www.infonegocio.com/pensionsanlorenzo  *Map 4,
B4, p252*  A friendly star of the old town near the *Bretxa* market.
Admirably, the well-priced, brightly decorated rooms come with
TV, fridge, kettle and piped radio. Some come with just a shower
and basin, others with bathroom. Internet access.  A quiet place,
but fills fast.

## Centro

**LL Hotel Maria Cristina**, C Oquendo 1, Centro,  **T** 943-437600,
**F** 943-437676, www.westin.com  *Map 4, C5, p252*  Tiny riverfront
hotel that's difficult to spot – if you're in orbit. Taking up an entire
block, its elegant sandstone bulk has cradled more celebrities than
you could drop a fork at. All the luxury and class you would expect,
and prices that boot other five-star hotels in to campsite class.

**L Hotel Europa**, C San Martín 52, Centro, **T** 943-470880,
**F** 943-471730, www.hotel-europa.com  *Map 4, F4, p252*  A hotel
with more frills than substance, near the beach. It's well-equipped
and has some nice fittings, but is rather overpriced.

**L Hotel Londres y Inglaterra**, C Zubieta 2, Centro,
**T** 943-440770, **F** 943-440491, www.hlondres.com  *Map 4, E4, p252*
Grand old beachfront hotel which is an emblem of the city's glory
days. Great location and good service – if royalty don't drop by as
often as they once did, no one is letting on.

**A Hotel Niza**, C Zubieta 56, Centro, **T** 943-426663, **F** 943-441251, www.hotelniza.com *Map 4, F3, p252* Slap bang on the beach, this hotel is an odd mixture of casual seaside and starchy formality. About half the rooms have views – it goes without saying that they are better than the others, some of which are noisy.

**C/B Hostal Alemana**, C San Martín 53, Centro, **T** 943-462544, **F** 943-461771, www.hostalalemana.com *Map 4, F3, p252* That rarest of beasts: an efficient modern hotel with warm personal service. Excellent value it has all the conveniences, plus some nice views and a pretty breakfast room.

**C/B Pensión Bellas Artes**, C Urbieta 64, Centro, **T** 943-474905. *Map 4, G5, p253* A well-run, well-decorated pensión near the Euskotren station.

**D Pensión San Martín**, C San Martín 10, Centro, **T** 943-428714. *Map 4, E5, p252* One of the better choices on this street. The comfy rooms have bathrooms and TV. Very handy for the train station/heavy bags combination.

**E Pensión Urkia**, C Urbieta 12, Centro, **T** 943-428123, and **E** Pensión La Perla, C Loiola 10, **T** 943-428123. *Map 4, E4, p252* Around the corner from each other, these are good places to stay near the new cathedral. Run by the same family, who can also locate some good rooms in private houses if full.

## Ondarreta

**AL Hotel Monte Igueldo**, Paseo del Faro 134, **T** 943-210211, **F** 943215028, www.monteigueldo.com *Map 5, B1, p254* Perched on Monte Igueldo, it's all about location here; most of the rooms offer a spectacular view, one way or another. It's hardly a peaceful retreat, as the summit is shared with a tacky amusement park.

**A Hotel Ezeiza**, Av Satrustegui 13, **T** 943-214311, **F** 943-214768, www.hotelezeiza.com *Map 5, C1, p254* Nicely situated at the peaceful western end of Ondarreta beach, this is a welcoming place with the added attraction of an excellent terrace bar.

**A Hotel La Galeria**, C Infanta Cristina 3, **T** 943-216077, **F** 943-211298, www.hotellagaleria.com *Map 5, D1, p254* Old fashioned plushness in this imposing sandstone hotel, guarded by a sphinx. Well located on a quiet street by the beach, this is better priced than it looks.

**La Sirena**, Paseo de Igueldo 25, **T** 943-310268, **F** 943-214090. *Map 5, D1, p254* Although it's far from central, San Sebastián's IH hostel is close to Ondarreta beach, and easily accessible by bus from town. Curfews, early check-outs, and school groups are the drawbacks.

**Camping Igueldo**, Paseo Padre Orkolaga 69, **T** 943-214502, **F** 943-280411. Open all year, this big San Sebastián campsite is set back from Ondarreta beach, behind Monte Igueldo.

### Gros

**C Pensión Aida**, C Iztueta 9, **T** 943-327800, **F** 943-326707, aida@pensionesconencanto.com *Map 4, C7, p252* A good base, and convenient for the station. The gleaming rooms are appealing, and breakfast in bed is a great way to start the day as you mean to continue.

**C Pensión Kursaal**, C Peña y Goñi 2, **T** 943-292666, **F** 943-297536,, www.pensionesconencanto.com *Map 4, B6, p252* A good place to stay, very near the beach. Big windows in attractive rooms with bathrooms and TV. Internet access.

## Southern Hills

**E Artola**, Barrio Santiago Mendi, Astigarraga, **T** 943-557296.
This welcoming and attractive house, in the heart of hilly cider
country, offers meals as well as kitchen facilities.

# East of San Sebastián

## Hondarribia and around

**AL Parador de Hondarribia**, Plaza de Armas 14, Hondarribia,
**T** 943-645500, **F** 943-642153.   Originally constructed in the 10th
century, then reinforced by Carlos V to resist French attacks. Behind
the beautiful martial façade is a hotel of considerable comfort and
delicacy, although the rooms don't reach the ornate standard set by
the public areas, which bristle with reminders of its military function.
A pretty courtyard and terrace are the highlights.

**A Hotel Obispo**, Plaza del Obispo s/n, Hondarribia, **T** 943-645400,
**F** 943-642386.   The old archbishop's palace is an ultra-characterful
place to stay; a beautiful building with nice views across the
Bidasoa. The rooms are well-equipped, although they don't quite
live up to the expectations set by the gorgeous façade.

**C Iketxe**, Barrio Arkoll, **T** 943-644391.   One of several *agroturismos*
around Hondarribia, this very pretty farmhouse is south west of
town, off the road to Irun, past the chapel of Santiagotxo.

**D Hostal Alvarez Quintero**, C Bernat Etxepare 2, Hondarribia,
**T** 943-642299.   A tranquil little place with a distinctly old-fashioned
air. The rooms are simple and reasonably priced compared to the
other options in town, but it is a little difficult to find. The entrance is
through an arch, on the roundabout by the tourist office.

**E Hostal Txoko-Goxoa**, C Murrua 22, Hondarribia.  A pretty little place on a peaceful, sunny street by the town walls. The bedrooms are smallish but homely, with flowers in the window boxes.

**Camping Faro de Higuer**, Paseo del Faro 58, Hondarribia, **T** 943-641008, **F** 943-640150.  One of two decent campsites, slightly closer to town, on the way to the lighthouse.

# West of San Sebastián

### Getaria and around

**D Gure Ametsa**, Orrua s/n, **T** 943-140077.  Off a backroad between Zumaia and Getaria, this friendly farmhouse is in a superb location, with views out the sea. Cheaper rooms without ensuite.

**D Pensión Txikipolit**, Plaza Musica s/n, Zarautz, **T** 943-835357, **F** 943-833731.  One of the best budget options, very well located in the old part of town. Comfy and characterful rooms.

**E Hostal Itxas-Gain**, C San Roque 1, Getaria, **T** 943-141033. Lovely, warm-hearted, overlooking the sea, with charming rooms. On the top floor there's a suite with a spa-bath. There's also a garden, which is a top place to chill in hot weather and a friendly dog.

**Gran Camping Zarautz,** Monte Talaimendi, Zarautz, **T** 943-831238, **F** 943-132486.  Massive campsite with the lot, open all year round, but depressingly packed in summer's dog days.

**Talaimendi,** Talaimendi s/n, Zarautz, **T** 943-830132.  Decent self-catering apartments, sleeping up to six. Cheaper in low season.

**Tomas,** Plaza Gurruchaga 12, Zumaia, **T** 943-861916.   Attractive apartments sleeping four, €48-72 depending on time of year.

# Vitoria/Gasteiz

---

### Casco Medieval

D **Hotel Desiderio**, C Colegio San Prudencio 2, **T** 945-251700, **F** 945-251722.   Welcoming hotel with comfy rooms with private bathroom, just out of the Casco Medieval.

G **Pensión Antonio**, C Cuchillería 66, Casco Medieval, **T** 945-268795. The cheapest place in town, with rooms at €9.70 per person with shared bathrooms. It's simple but decent. At this price it's pretty popular, so ring a couple of days beforehand.

---

### New town

L **Hotel Canciller Ayala**, C Ramón y Cajal 5, **T** 945-130000, **F** 945-133505.   Located on Parque de la Florida, this four-star hotel doesn't make the most of its setting. While it's got facilities coming out of its ears, you get the feeling that if you ain't there for a convention, you ain't nobody.

L **Hotel Ciudad de Vitoria**, Portal de Castilla 8, **T** 945-141100, **F** 945-143616.   Massive four-star hotel, situated on the edge of central Vitoria, where character starts to make way for "lifestyle". It's airy and pleasant, with good facilities, including a gym and sauna. The major draw is the incredible weekend rates, with doubles from €63, less than half the weekday rate.

A **Hotel Almoneda**, C Florida 7, **T** 945-154084, **F** 945-154686. Attractively situated a few paces from the lovely Parque de la

Florida, this hotel has reasonable rooms with a rustic touch, much nicer than the stuffy lobby suggests. Significantly cheaper at weekends. Breakfast included.

C **Hotel Páramo**, C General Alava 11, **T** 945-140240, **F** 945-140492. Strangely located in a shopping arcade, this hotel has snug rooms with simple but attractive furniture. Plenty of facilities and breakfast included.

D **Hotel Dato**, C Eduardo Dato 28, **T** 945-147230, **F** 945-232320. While it might not be to everyone's taste, this hotel is a treasury of *clásico* statues, mirrors, and general plushness, in a comfortable rather than stuffy way. Its rooms are exceptional value too; all are pretty, with excellent facilities, and some have balconies or *miradores* (enclosed balconies).

E **Pensión Araba II**, C Florida 25, **T** 945-232588. A good base in central Vitoria. Clean and comfortable rooms with or without bathroom. Parking spaces available (€6).

F **Casa 400**, C Florida 46, **T** 945-233887. At this price don't expect many facilities, but still, this is clean, comfortable and cheerfully run.

**Albergue Juvenil**, C Escultor Isaac Diáz s/n, **T** 945-148100. Vitoria's youth hostel is about 10-minutes' walk from the station on the other side of the railway line from the centre of town.

**Camping Ibaya**, Ctra 102, **T** 945-147620. The closest campsite to Vitoria, a few kilometres past the basilica at Armentia.

# Alava/Araba

A **Parador de Argómaniz**, Carretera N1 Km 363, **T** 945-293200, **F** 945-293287. www.parador.es 12 km east of Vitoria, just off the N1, the hamlet of Argómaniz is dominated by a parador set in a Renaissance palace. It's a tranquil setting with good views over the surrounding countryside. Napoleon slept here before the disastrous battle of Vitoria. The older part of the building is lovely, and contains the restaurant (a beautiful area under the wooden roof) and bar. The rooms, in a more recent annexe, don't reach the same standard, but are reasonable value and have all mod-cons. As with all paradors, check the website as there are often excellent special offers. The restaurant, open to non guests, has a Basque-ish *menú* for €22.84, as well as a daily *plato*. A cab to/from Vitoria costs about €15.

D **Merino**, Plaza de San Juan 3, East Alava, **T** 945-300052.
Nice if slightly overpriced rooms with bathroom and TV, on the main plaza above a bar/restaurant which is the best eating option in town. It is advisable to book ahead.

D **Guzurtegi**, Barrio La Plazuela s/n, West Alava, **T** 945-399438. A very pretty, hospitable farmhouse with attractive and comfortable rooms not far from Orduña, offering full and half board.

E **Mendiaxpe,** Barrio Salsamendi 22, East Alava, **T** 945-304212.
Cleverly located in the wooded foothills of the Sierra de Urkilla, this is a superb base for walking in the area. Near the town of Araia, connected by bus to Vitoria, the house has kitchen facilities available for guests' use.

**Camping Angosto**, Ctra Villanañe-Angosto, West Alava, **T** 94-7353271. On the edge of the Valderejo National Park, this campsite is quite out of the way, but has excellent facilities and makes a good base for walking, canoeing and horseriding. There are bungalows, a bar/restaurant and a swimming pool. It can get pretty busy with families during summer.

# La Rioja Alavesa

**A Castillo El Collado**, Paseo El Collado 1, Laguardia,
**T** 945-621200, F 945-621022.   Decorated in plush style,
this mansion at the north end of the old town has a good,
reasonably priced restaurant.

**A Posada Mayor de Migueloa**, C Mayor 20, Laguardia,
**T** 945-621175, **F** 945-621022.   A beautifully decorated Spanish
country house, with lovely furniture and a peaceful atmosphere.
The restaurant is of a similar standard.

**B Hotel Antigua Bodega de Don Cosme Palacio**, Carretera
Elciego s/n, Laguardia.   **T** 945-621195, **F** 945-600210,
antiguabodega@cosmepalacio.com  A wine-lover's delight.
The old Palacio *bodega* has been converted into a charming hotel
and restaurant, adjacent to the winery. The sunny rooms are
named after grape varietals, and come with a free half-bottle.
Air-conditioned to cope with the fierce summer heat, most rooms
feature views over the vines and mountains beyond. Reasonable
rates too.

**E Larretxori**, Portal de Páganos s/n, Laguardia, **T/F** 945-600763,
larretxori@euskalnet.net   Just outside the city walls, with excellent
views over the area.

Eating is one of the things the Basques do best. Most of Spain grudgingly concedes that Basque cuisine is the peninsula's best, the San Sebastián twilight shimmers with Michelin stars, and chummy all-male txokos gather in private to swap recipes and cook up feasts in members-only kitchens. But what strikes the visitor first are the pintxos, a stunning range of bartop snacks that in many cases seem too pretty to put your teeth in (see box, p152). Basque cuisine is based on seafood, with that Spanish staple the merluza (hake) featuring alongside bacalao, dried salt cod that is definitely an acquired taste but occasionally is delicious. Ingredients used to spice these and other seafoods and meats are typically garlic, peppers and olive oil. See the food glossary for a more detailed run-down on Basque edibles and potables. Eating hours are later than most of Europe, although not as much as in other parts of Spain. Lunch is normally served between 1330-1530, although this runs later at weekends.

**Price**

**Eating codes**

€€€   30 and over
€€    15-30
€     15 and under
Price codes refer to a two-course meal, excluding drinks and service

Most restaurants offer a *menú del día*, a three-course meal with wine; this is usually unremarkable but excellent value, costing between €5 and €10. A handful of places offer a similar menú in the evening too. At about seven or eight, while northern Europe is halfway through dinner, everyone is on the street, strolling up and down in the paseo, ducking into bars for a swift drink and a *pintxo*, or sitting on a terraza somewhere nursing a coffee or a vermouth.

Most restaurants don't open in the evening until 2030, but most people won't eat until 2000, later at weekends. On weeknights the Basque country shuts down fairly early, but at weekends the *pintxo* bars and restaurants keep buzzing well into the *madrugada*.

Bilbao's Casco Viejo is undoubtedly the best place to head for *pintxos* and evening drinking, the best areas being the Plaza Nueva and around the Siete Calles. There's another concentration of bars on Avenida Licenciado Poza and the smaller C García Rivero off it. The narrow Calle Ledesma, a street back from Gran Vía, is a popular place to head for after-work snacks and drinks. There are some good restaurants in the Casco Viejo, but also plenty of options scattered through the New Town and Deusto.

# Bilbao/Bilbo

## Casco Viejo

€€€ **Harrobia**, C Perro 2, **T** 94-6790090.  *Map 1, E2, p247*
Warm but elegant restaurant in the heart of the old town dealing with traditionally Basque and Spanish ingredients presented in a fairly modern style.

€€€ **Victor**, Plaza Nueva 2, **T** 944-151678.  *Map 1, D2, p247*
A quality upstairs restaurant with an elegant but relaxed atmosphere. This is a top place to try Bilbao's signature dish, *bacalao al pil-pil*, or the restaurant's variation on it, and there's an excellent wine selection. Conforms to the general Iberian rule of decreasing vegetables with increasing price.

€€€ **Victor Montes**, Plaza Nueva 8, **T** 944-155603.  *Map 1, C3, p247* Very popular *pintxo* bar with a small restaurant.
If you can shoulder your way to the bar in the evening, you'll find that not a square inch is free of posh bites. Equally impressive is the collection of whiskies behind the bar.

€€ **Aji Colorado**, C Barrencalle 5, **T** 944-152209.  *Map 1, F3, p247* A small and friendly Peruvian restaurant in the heart of the Casco Viejo. Discover the taste of ceviche, delicious seafood 'cooked' by being marinated in lemon or lime juice – flavour and then some.

€€ **Berton**, C Jardines 11, **T** 944-167035.  *Map1, E2, p246*
The hanging jamones and bunches of grapes define this cheerful bar, which has top-notch hammy pintxos and raciones and some quality wines by the glass. Packed at weekends.

€€ **Kasko**, C Santa María, **T** 944-160311.   *Map 1, E2, p247*   With funky decor inspired by the fish and high-class new Basque food, this is one of Casco Viejo's best restaurants, and has a very reasonable evening *menú* for €16.60, sometimes accompanied by a pianist.

€€ **La Deliciosa**, C Jardines 1, **T** 944-163590.   *Map 1, E2, p247* Modern decor and contemporary Basque cuisine in a new restaurant whose bright interior contrasts with the dark Casco Viejo alleys. The set dinner at 16 is good value. One of the few in the Casco to be open for Sunday and Monday dinner.

€€ **Xukela**, C Perro 2, **T** 944-159772.   *Map 1, E2, p247*   A very social bar on a very social street. Attractive *pintxos*, some good sit-down food, and a clientele upending glasses of Rioja at a competitive pace until comparatively late.

€ **Bar Irintzi**, C Santa María 8.   *Map 1, E1, p247* *Pintxos* are an art form in this excellent bar; there´s a superb array of imaginative snacks, carefully labelled, freshly made and compassionately priced.

€ **Café-Bar Bilbao**, Plaza Nueva 6, **T** 944-151671.   *Map 1, D3, p247*   A sparky place with top service and a selection of some of the better pintxos to be had around the old town.

€ **Café Lamiak**, C Pelota 8, **T** 944-161765.   *Map 1, F2, p247* A relaxed two-floor forum, the sort of place a literary genre, pressure group, or world-famous funk band might start out. Mixed crowd.

€ **Gatz**, C Santa María 10, **T** 944-154861.   *Map 1, E1, p247* A convivial bar with some of Casco's better *pintxos*, which happily spills on to the street at weekends.

€ **Jaunak**, C Somera 10, **T** 94 4159979.   *Map 1, E4, p247*   One of a few friendly Basque bars on this street, with a range of *bocadillos*.

### ▶ Pintxos

Wherever you go in the Basque country, you'll be confronted and tempted by a massive array of food across the top of bars. Many bars serve up very traditional fare: slices of tortilla (potato omelette) or *pulgas de jamón* (small rolls with cured ham). Other bars, enthused by 'new Basque' cuisine, take things further and dedicate large parts of their day to creating miniature food sculptures using more esoteric ingredients.

The key factor is that they're all meant to be eaten. You can ask the bartender or simply help yourself to what you fancy, making sure to remember what you've had for the final reckoning. If you can't tell what something is, ask ( *de que es*?). Pintxos usually cost about €1 to €1.20 depending on the bar.

€ **Rio Oja**, C Perro 4, **T** 944-150871. *Map 1, E2, p247* Another good option on this street, specializing in bubbling Riojan stews and Basque fish dishes, most served in big casseroles at the bar.

€ **Rotterdam**, C Perro 6, **T** 94 4162165. *Map 1, E2, p247* Uncomplicated restaurant with a *simpático* boss. Decent lunch for €7.

### Riverbank

€€€ **Guggenheim**, Av Abandoibarra 2, **T** 944-239333. *Metro: Moyúa. Map 2, B6, p248* A good all-round option. The restaurant is run by one of San Sebastián's top chefs, with the quality and prices to match, but there's a first-rate *menú del día* for €12.39. The furniture is Gehry's work, but the carpark view, disappointing. No bookings are taken for the *menú*, served (slowly) from 1330 on a first-come basis. The cafés do a fine line in croissants, coffee and *pintxos*; Gallery 104 has more seating and a nice view over the river.

€€ **Mesón Los Angeles**, C Cristo 12, **T** 944-460676.
*Metro: Casco Viejo.* *Map 2, A11, p248* Tucked up a side street
behind the Ayuntamiento, this restaurant does some no-nonsense
and very good fish and meat grills. Good menú del día.

€ **Café Boulevard**, C Arenal 3, **T** 944-153128. *Metro: Casco
Viejo.* *Map 2, C12, p249* Fans of Art-Deco will not want to miss this
refurbished defender of the style, unchanged from the early 20th
century, when it was Bilbao's beloved 'meeting place'. Founded in
1871, there are plenty of seats, good breakfasts, coffees, *pintxos*
and weekday lunchtime *platos combinados*.

€ **El Kiosko del Arenal**, Muelle del Arenal s/n. *Metro: Casco
Viejo.* *Map 2, C12, p249* Elegant, cool café under the bandstand in
the Arenal. Plenty of outdoor tables overlooking the river. Damned
decent coffee.

### El Ensanche

€€€ **Bermeo**, C Ercilla 37, **T** 944-705700. *Metro: Indautxu.*
*Map 2, G7, p249* Although it's the restaurant of the *Hotel Ercilla*,
this stands on its own feet as one of the best places to dine in
Bilbao. Specializing in seafood, which is done in both typical
Basque styles and some innovative modern styles.

€€€ **Guria**, Gran Vía 66, **T** 944-415780. *Metro: San Mamés.*
*Map 2, F5, p248* One of Bilbao's top restaurants, with a sombrely
elegant atmosphere, its stock-in-trade is *bacalao*. After tasting it
here, you may forgive the codfish for all of the bad dishes that have
been produced with it in other kitchens and factories around the
world; if not, you can write *bacalao* off for good. There are *menús
de degustacíon* for €41 and €59, and a *menú del dia* for €28.40.
Out with these, count on €60 a head minimum, more if you
forsake the fish for the meat, which is tender and toothsome.

€€ **Asador Jauna**, C Juan Zunzunegui 7, **T** 944-417381.  *Metro: San Mamés.*  *Map 2, H8, p249*  Despite its characterless location, this is a good choice for the carnivore. The menu is a lot fuller than at a lot of *asadors*, with plenty of fish, as well as venison, duck, and other departures from the sirloin and T-bone hierarchy. It's fairly pricey but has a good atmosphere when busy, and they usually offer an uninspired daytime *menú* for around €11-14.

€€ **Etxeko Tavern**, C Henao 27, **T** 944-235305.  *Metro: Moyúa.*  *Map 2, D7, p248*  Decent new town bar and restaurant specializing in *pintxos*, *jamón*, and *bacalao* dishes. While the main dishes are good, the lunch *menú* isn't a bargain at €11.

€€ **La Barraca**, C Bertendona 6, **T** 944-150818.  *Metro: Abando.*  *Map 2, E10, p249*  If you fancy *paella* this might be the place to come; they certainly take it seriously, with 12 different rices.

€€ **Nicolás**, C Ledesma 10, **T** 944-240737.  *Metro: Abando.*  *Map 2, C11, p249*  A fairly old-fashioned little bar and restaurant with a small but delicious selection of nibbles as well as a good dining room.

€€ **Primera Instancia**, Alameda Mazarredo 6, **T** 944-236545.  Metro: Abando.  *Map 2, C10, p248*  Buzzy modern bar that's upmarket but far from pretentious. Small restaurant with a €19.90 *menú de degustacíon*. Check out the snazzy umbrella wrapper.

€€ **Serantes and Serantes II**, C Licenciado Poza 16, Alameda Urquijo 51, **T** 944-102066.  *Metro: Indautxu.*  *Map 2, F8, p249*  These *marisquerías* are not as pricy as their high reputation would suggest, with fish dishes around the €18 mark. It´s very fresh, and the chefs have the confidence to let the flavours of the seafood hold their own. Go for the daily special – usually excellent, or tackle some *cigalas*, the four-wheel-drive of the prawn world, equipped with *pincers* (sometimes called Dublin Bay prawns in English).

€€ **Sidrería Tártalo**, C Alameda Rekalde 69, **T** 944-100903. *Euskotren: Zabálburu, Metro: Indautxu.* Map 2, H10, p249  A cheerful modern restaurant named for the feared cyclops of the Basque mountains and consequently devoted to providing some seriously giant-sized meals. Drink your fill from the vats of cider…

€€ **Taberna Zara**, C Pablo Picasso 2, **T** 944-439242.  *Euskotren: Zabálburu, Metro: Indautxu.* Map 2, H11, p249  Near Plaza Zabalburu, this restaurant, decorated with a tribal vibe, has decent-value *menús*. Steak and seafood are what they do best.

€ **Artajo**, C Ledesma 7, **T** 944-248596.  *Metro: Abando.* Map 2, D10, p249  Uncomplicated, candid bar with homely wooden tables and chairs and good traditional snacks of *tortilla* and *pulgas de jamón*. Famous for its *tigres*, mussels in spicy tomato sauce.

€ **Café Iruña**, Jardines de Albia s/n, **T** 944-237021.  *Metro: Abando.* Map 2, C10, p249  This noble old establishment on the Jardines de Albia is approaching its century in style. Well refurbished, the large building is divided into a smarter café space with wood panelling in neo-Moorish style, and a tiled bar with some good *pintxos* – including lamb kebabs sizzling on the barbie.

€ **Café La Granja**, Plaza Circular 3.  **T** 944-230813.  *Metro: Abando.* Map 2, C11, p249  Another spacious old Bilbao café, opened in 1926. Its high ceilings and long bar are designed to cope with the lively throng that comes in throughout the day. Plenty of attractive Art Nouveau fittings and good food. Closes fairly early.

€ **Café Mistyk**, C Ercilla 1, **T** 944-236342.  *Metro: Moyúa.* Map 2, B8, p249  A theatre cafe on the corner of Mazarredo. There are weekly shows on a Tuesday or Thursday night; these vary from flamenco to comedy and are free, but have a *consumo mínimo* (minimum consumption) of €3 per person.

**Best**

**Pintxos that stand out and get counted**

- Irintzi, Casco Viejo, Bilbao, p151.
- Garbola, San Sebastián, p167.
- La Cuchara de San Telmo, San Sebastián, p165.
- Bar Garriti, San Sebastián ,p165.
- Saburdi, Vitoria, p172.

€ **Café Monaco**, Alameda de Recalde 34, **T** 944-238684.
*Metro: Moyúa. Map 2, E7, p249* A good choice for breakfast, with
quality coffee, *pintxos* and a host with a soft spot for Athletic Bilbao.

€ **Despacho**, C García Rivero 2, **T** 944-413570. *Metro:
Indautxu. Map 2, G7, p248* Very handy bar for workers in the area,
who can tell their boss that they were 'in the office' all afternoon.

€ **Buddha Bar**, C Ayala 1, **T** 944-157136. *Metro: Abando.
Map 2, D11, p249* Tucked away behind the *Corte Inglés* is this
modern Asian fusion restaurant. Choices are mainly centred
around Japanese and Thai, which are done well. There's a good
value *menú* for €8.50, day and night, Monday to Thursday.

€ **Don Chufo**, C Iparraguirre 17, **T** 944-235499. *Metro:
Moyúa. Map 2, D7, p249* A place that crops up in laptop ads, with
dark glass and sleek furniture. Good €9 lunch, within striking
distance of the Guggenheim, and popular with business workers.

€ **Garibolo**, C Fernández del Campo 7, **T** 944-273255. *Metro:
Moyúa. Map 2, G10, p249* While at first glance Bilbao doesn't
seem large enough a Spanish city to sustain a vegetarian restaurant, the colourful Garibolo packs 'em in, particularly for its €9
lunch special. A range of Asian-inspired dishes as well as
recommendable stuffed eggplant/aubergine and organic wines.

€ **Guggen Restaurant**, Alameda Recalde 5, **T** 944-248491.
*Metro: Moyúa.* *Map 2, C7, p249* Despite its name and proximity to the
museum, this restaurant is a fairly authentic workers' lunch den, with
an unspectacular but enjoyable *menú del día* for €6.15, and an
upgraded version for those who don't want to pay as little as that.

€ **Juantxu**, C Licenciado Poza 39. *Metro: Indautxu.* *Map 2, G6,*
*p248* Decorated with a half-hearted nautical theme, this friendly
bar is notable for its strangely addictive mini-hamburger *pintxos*.

€ **La Galea**, C Rodríguez Arias 71, **T**944-425507. Metro: San
Mamés. *Map 2, G4, p248* A restaurant which manages to over-
come the ugly architecture in this part of town with well-placed
creepers and an excellent *menú del día* which is a treat for €8.50.

€ **Lekeitio**, C Diputación 1, **T** 944-239240. *Metro: Moyúa.* *Map 2,*
*D9, p248* An attentive bar with a fanstastic selection of after-work
eats. Good variety of fishy and seafoody *pintxos*, and *tortilla*.

€ **Okela**, C García Rivero 8, **T** 944-415937. *Metro: Indautxu.* *Map*
*2, G7, p249* A modern bar popular with the office crowd and dominated by a huge signed photo of the footballer Joseba Etxebarria
in full stride for Athletic Bilbao. Nice *pintxos*.

€ **Taberna Taurina**, C Ledesma 5, **T** 94 4241381. *Metro:*
*Abando.* *Map 2, C11, p248* A tiny old-time tiles 'n' sawdust bar
which is packed top-to-bottom with bullfighting memorabilia. It's
fascinating to browse the old pictures which convey something of
the sport's noble side. The *tortilla* here also commands respect.

€ **Zuretzat**, C Iparraguirre 7, **T** 944-248505. *Metro: Moyúa.* *Map*
*2, C6, p248* A decent bar decked out with prints of ships from the
golden days of the ocean liner, as well as the hard hats of the workers who built the *Guggenheim*. Prices reflect passing tourist trade.

€ **Zuripot**, Cnr C Licenciado Poza and Av Dr Areilza. *Metro: Indautxu. Map 2, G6, p248* A solid corner choice decorated with clowns and strange ceramic figures. Suberb, if skimpy, *tortilla*.

## Deusto

€€ **Casa Vasca**, Av Lehendakari Aguirre 13-15. **T** 944-483980. *Map 2, E1, p248* A Deusto institution – the front bar has a good selection of posh-*pintxos* and a couple of comfortable nooks to settle down with a slightly pricy drink. Behind is a restaurant that serves pretty authentic Basque cuisine in generous portions.

€€ **Deustoarrak**, Av Madariaga 9. **T** 944-751581. *Map 2, E1, p248* This steak 'n' fish restaurant on Deusto's liveliest street is decorated in mock-Gothic style with suits of armour guarding the stairs. The *menú del día* is good value at €8.40.

€€ **Oriotarra**, C Blas de Otero 30, Deusto, **T** 944-470830. *Map 2, E1, p248* A classy *pintxo* bar that has won an award for the best bartop snack in Bilbao. A round of applause for the pig's ear millefeuille.

€ **Txoko del Vino**, C Blas de Otero 26, Deusto, **T** 944-763564. *Map 2, E1, p248* A bar that couldn't be less glamorous or more authentic, with cheap wine and hams that might have been cured by the cigar smoke. Worth a look as a contrast.

## Portugalete, Getxo and the beaches

€€€ **Cubita Kaia**, Muelle de Arriluze 10-11, **T** 944-600103. *Metro: Neguri.* A highly acclaimed restaurant with views over the water from Getxo's marina. People have been known to kill for the *cigalas* (Dublin bay prawns) turned out by young modern chef Alvaro Martínez. Not to be confused with another restaurant named *Cubita* next to the windmill above Arrigunaga beach.

**★ Dishes to make a Basque of you**

**Best**

- **Bacalao al pil-pil**  Originally eaten during the Carlist siege of Bilbao, the sauce is something of a phenomenon, suddenly turning thick and yellow for no apparent reason.
- **Kokotxas**  Though eating fish cheeks may sound like a poor excuse for a meal, they're usually delicious.
- **Alubias de Tolosa**  The Rolls-Royce of beans is best served with pickled cabbage and lumps of meat. *Pochas a la Riojana* are another favourite bean dish.
- **Txangurro relleno**  Spider crab blended with fish, tomato, onion, and spices and served in its shell. Supreme.
- **Idiazabal con membrillo**  The Basque sheepmilk cheese packs a punch and is superbly offset by the sweet quince jelly.

€€€ **Jolastoki**, Av Leioa 24, **T** 944-912031.  *Metro: Neguri.*  Decorated in classy but homely country mansion style, *Jolastoki* is a house of good repute throughout Euskadi. Definitely traditional in character, dishes such as *caracoles en salsa vizcaína* (snails), and *liebre* (hare) are the sort of treats that give Basque cuisine its lofty reputation.

€€ **Karola Etxea**, C Aretxondo 22, **T** 944-600868.  *Metro: Algorta.*  Perfectly situated in a quiet lane above the old port. It's a good place to try some fish; there are usually a few available, such as *txitxarro* (scad) or *besugo* (sea bream). The *kokotxas* (cheeks and throats of hake in sauce) are also delicious.

€€ **Asador Goietz**, C Aretxondo 14, **T** 944-603883.  *Metro: Algorta.*  Also in the area of the old port, this restaurant specializes in grilling fish over open coals. As well as this, there's a good number of different crabs on offer to test your taste buds.

€€ **El Refugio**, Algortako Etorbidea 90, **T** 944-601209. *Metro: Algorta.* A cute narrow hideaway on the main street through Getxo, with a good selection of homely Basque dishes and some good seafood.

€ **Restaurante Vegetariano**, Algortako Etorbidea 100, **T** 944-601762. *Metro: Algorta.* A good vegetarian option with a salad buffet, a *menú del día* for €8, and an upbeat attitude.

€ **Zodiako's**, C Euskal Herria s/n (corner of Telletxe), **T** 944-604059**.** *Metro: Algorta.* This squiggly bar in the heart of Getxo is one of the area's best, with a terrace, *pintxos*, and service with a smile.

# Inland

## Gernika

€€ **Lezika,** Cuevas de Santamamiñe, Kortezubi, **T** 94-6252975. The whole of Vizcaya seems to descend on the beer garden here at weekends with kids and dogs in tow; the restaurant is better value than the meagre *raciones* on offer at the bar.

€ **Arrien**, C Eriabarrena 1, **T**94-6258551. Overlooking the flowery Jardines de El Ferial, this terraced restaurant/bar has a very acceptable *menú del día* for €7.21 and various other set meals from €10 as well as *à la carte* selections.

€ **Parra Taberna**, Elorrio. A peaceful bar with tables on the main square and a beautiful glass and stone interior.

### Beans

For many in the English speaking world the word beans is about as far as it gets from the word gourmet. School dinners, tail-between-the-legs pre-payday trips to the supermarket for the 2p special on tins of no-name sludge, the barely warm gut-bombs at dodgy B&B.

In Spain, however, they are taken seriously, especially in the Basque lands. There are more types of beans than you'd care to name. Brought back from the Americas, their high energy values made them a perfect staple, but they have greater significance. In Alava, *pochas* are an esteemed dish, soft, whiteish, and picked very young. Vitoria rates its own creations of *habas* (broadbeans) very highly, while beans *a la Vizcaína* go down a treat in Bilbao.

The Brazil of the bean world cup, however, is Tolosa. *Alubias de Tolosa* are to *Heinz* baked beans what caviar is to grit. Small and dark red in colour, they are traditionally cooked in clay pots. Tolosans will tell you that the beans only taste at their best when cooked in hard Tolosan water. Tolosan beans have a *Denominación de Origen* much like wine, and there's an annual contest among the official growers of them. They are traditionally eaten with pork, *morcilla* (blood sausage), and cabbage. It's a delicious winter warmer if done properly (if not, it can be tasteless), but it's heavy going in the sweaty summer heat…

## Oñati/Arantzazu

€ **Arkupe**, Plaza del los Fueros 9, **T** 943-781699. A good bar/restaurant on Oñati's main square, with a variety of cheap *raciones* and *platos*, and a focus of the early evening, outdoor drinking scene.

# The Basque Coastline

## Bermeo and Mundaka

€€ **Asador Bodegon**, Kepa Deuna 1, Mundaka,
**T** 94-6876353.  Mundaka's best restaurant, despite a slight air of
'we know what the tourists want'. Meat and, especially fresh fish
are grilled to perfection over the coals. Try the home-made
*patxarán*, a liqueur made from sloe berries.

€€ **Gaztelu Begi**, Carretera San Pelaio 86, between Bakio and
Bermeo, **T** 94-6194924.  This roadside hotel above San Juan de
Gaztelugatxe, is a good spot for a meal or a drink while waiting for
the bus. Good views, and reasonable fish at about €15.

€ **Batzokia**, *on Mundaka's main square*. The €9.90 *menú del día*
can be a good opportunity to try the local catch at a discount.

€ **Ereperi**, San Pelaio s/n, between Bakio and Bermeo,
**T** 94-6194065.  A good restaurant overlooking San Juan de
Gaztelagutxe, with a superb terrace and a cheap lunch *menú*.

€ **Hotel El Puerto**, Portu Kalea 1, Mundaka, **T** 94-6876725.  The bar
below this hotel is Mundaka's best, overlooking the  harbour.

## Lekeitio and around

€€€ **Oxangoiti Jauregia,** C Gamarra 2, Lekeitio, **T** 94-6843151.
A fairly expensive restaurant in an historic building next to the
*ayuntamiento*. Smart wooden interior, a craft shop, and tasty
seafood (how did you guess?) at fairly stiff prices.

€€ **Emperatriz Zita**, Santa Elena Etorbidea s/n, Lekeitio, **T** 94-6842655. The restaurant in this seafront hotel is well-priced.

€€ **Eretegia Joxe Manuel**, C Sabino Arana 23, Ondarroa, **T** 94- 6830104. Although it does a range of other appetising dishes, the big charcoal grill outside this restaurant caters to carnivores with large appetites. Forget quarter-pounders; here the steaks approach the kilogram mark and are very tasty. About €30 a head.

€€ **Hotel Beitia**, Av Pascual Abaroa 25, Lekeitio, **T** 94-6840111. The restaurant is a much better bet than the hotel, with high-quality seafood, and a pleasant patio.

€€ **Kaia**, Txatxo kaia 5, Lekeitio, **T** 94-6840284. One of many harbourside restaurants, this serves fairly upmarket but tasty fish.

€€ **Restaurante Zapirain**, Igualdegui 5, Lekeitio, **T** 94-6840255. A fish restaurant which is popular with Lekeitians as well as visitors. Fairly traditional in style and welcoming in manner.

€ **Hotel Zubieta**, Portal de Atea, Lekeitio, **T** 94-6843030. The lively café bar in this beautifully restored coachhouse is an excellent spot for a chat and a beverage in uplifting surroundings.

€ **Sutargi**, Nasa Kalea 11, Ondarroa, **T** 94-6832258. A popular bar with a good-value restaurant upstairs with main dishes, €9-10.

€ **Talako bar**. Above the fisherman's co-operative on the harbour. A great spot for one of Lekeitio's rainy days, with a pool table, and a 180° view of the harbour, town, and beaches.

€ **Txalupa**, Txatxo kaia 7, Lekeitio, **T** 94-6841386. While Lekeitio isn't as out-and-out Basque as Ondarroa, this bar keeps the Basque rock pumping, and does a range of simple snacks.

# ★ San Sebastián/Donostia

The best places for *pintxos* are in the Parte Vieja, which teems with bars. Gros is a quieter but tasty option. Restaurants abound in the old town too, although some of the best are further afield, in the new town or outside the city limits.

## Parte Vieja

€€€ **Casa Nicolasa**, C Aldamar 4, **T** 943-421762. *Map 4, B5, p252* This simple and gracious second floor dining room is the setting for one of the city's best restaurants. The emphasis is on seafood – the *almejas* (small clams) with trout roe are superb – and the service is restrained and attentive.

€€€ **Panier Fleuri**, Paseo Salamanca 2, **T** 943-424205. *Map 4, B5, p252* A bright and airy split-level restaurant with a French-inspired menu and an emphasis on fresh market produce and charcoal grilled meats.

€€€ **Urepel**, Paseo Salamanca 3, **T** 943-424040. *Map 4, B5, p252* A long and brooding restaurant with a fairly Spanish feel. The food is lighter, and the highlight is an elegantly treated shellfish. A good wine list accompanies the classy nosh.

€€ **Barbarin**, C Puerto 21, **T** 943-421886. *Map 4, B3, p252* A well-priced restaurant specialising in local seafood. The *rollitos de txangurro*, fried crab rolls, are especially tempting.

€€ **Casa Gandarias**, C 31 de Agosto 25, **T** 943-428106. *Map 4, B3, p252* A busy bar near the Santa María church with a pricy adjoining restaurant. The *pintxos* are good, but you virtually need a retina scan to use the bathroom.

€€ **Ganbara**, C San Jeronimo 21, **T** 943-422575. *Map 4, B3, p252* A fairly upmarket bar and *asador* with a worthwhile array of *pintxos* to accompany the cheerfully poured wine.

€ **Barandiaran**, Alameda del Boulevard 28, **T** 943-429796. *Map 4, C3, p252* Despite its location, this is a very authentic café with a loyal local following drinking strong coffee and tumblers of wine.

€ **Café del Boulevard**, Alameda del Boulevard 4. *Map 4, B4, p252* Good spot for brekkie or an evening drink and proof that Irish pubs don't have a monopoly on interesting bric-a-brac in these parts.

€ **Bar Garriti**, C San Juán 8. *Map 4, B4, p252* An unglamorous bar with an impressive spread of pintxos during the day and early evening.

€ **La Cepa**, C 31 de Agosto 7, **T** 943-426394. *Map 4, A4, p252* Perenially and deservedly popular bar lined with hams and featuring the head of a particularly large *toro* on the wall. Good atmosphere and *pintxos* and *raciones* to match.

€ **La Cuchara de San Telmo**, C 31 de Agosto 28 (back), **T** 943-420840. *Map 4, A4, p252* An extraordinary bar alongside the museum, with made-to-order gourmet dishes in miniature, for around €1.50-€2.50. Original and inspiring!

€ **Txalupa**, C Calbetón 3, **T** 943-429875. *Map 4, B4, p252* The restaurant under this bar does a decent *menú del día* for €9.50, which rises to €12 at weekends. Standard but tasty Basque fare.

€ **Tximista**, Plaza Constitución 10. *Map 4, B4, p252* A pocket-sized bar in this attractive square, with excellent snacks, particularly seafood.

**Eating and drinking**

## Centro

€€ **Café de la Concha**, Paseo de la Concha s/n, **T** 943-473600.
*Map 4, F2, 252*   A pretty place to stop for a coffee or a glass of wine
during a stroll along the beach. Decent restaurant with good views.

€€ **Iruaritz**, Av Libertad 40, **T** 943-433332.  *Map 4, D4, p253*
Historic café/bar with a genteel San Sebastián crowd. A *salón* atmosphere, with regular dancing exhibitions and attractive stained glass
behind the bar. The restaurant does *menús* for €10.80 and €15.03.

€€ **Oquendo**, C Oquendo 8, **T** 943-420932.  *Map 4, C5, p252*
A good, fairly formal restaurant near *Hotel Maria Cristina*, serving a
range of fresh fish for around €18 a plate. There is some good
bartop eating, and the photo wall from the San Sebastián Film
Festival is great for testing your silver-screen knowledge.

## Ondarreta

€€ **Restaurante San Martín**, Plazoleta Funicular, **T** 943-214084.
Next to the Igueldo funicular, this pretty house-on-a-hill is a restaurant specializing in fish and the odd game-bird. Outdoor eating and
great views from the dining room.

## Gros

€€€ **Kursaal Restaurant**, Av Zurriola 1, **T** 943-003162.
*Map 4, A6, p252*  Another restaurant overseen by top local chef
Martín Berasategui, this is attractively set in the Kursaal and features the most modern of Basque *nouvelle cuisine*. For the quality
on offer, it's not too pricey; you can eat well for around €50 a
head, and there are *menús de degustación* for €32.45 and €40.90
(no drinks), as well as a daytime one for €33.05 all inclusive.

There is also a café, which is an excellent spot for an early evening *pintxo* and drink, with superb views over the rivermouth and sea.

€ **Aloña Berri**, C Bermingham 24, **T** 943-290818.  *Map 4, A8, p252*  It's surprising the staff don't weep when a customer wolfs a *pintxo*, so much effort seems to have gone into making them pretty (and tasty).

€ **Bar Ondarra**, Av de la Zurriola 16.   Opposite the Kursaal exhibition centre, this is a decent bar with a street level and an underground den featuring regular live jazz and soul. Good *pintxos*.

€ **Bergara**, C General Artetxe 8, **T** 943-275026.  *Map 4, B8, p252*  Attractive Gros bar with stone and leaf exterior and wooden tables to eat and drink off.

€ **Garbola**, Paseo Colon 11, **T** 943-285019.  *Map 4, B7, p252*   A local legend in its own *pintxo*-time for its scrumptious mushroom creations and *caipirinhas*, this Gros bar also offers more unusual snacks, such as kangaroo and shark.

## Southern Hills

€€€ **Zuberoa**, Bº Iturriotz 8, **T** 943-491228.  *Closed Sun night and Mondays.*  Outside San Sebastián, near the town of Oiartzun/Oyarzun, is the lair of top chef Hilario Arbelaitz and his brothers. Actually it's far from being a lair, rather an attractive stone farmhouse with a wooden porch and terrace. Although it's very debatable whether the organ is qualified to make such a sweeping judgement, it has been named 10th- best restaurant in the world by the *International Herald Tribune*. Arbelaitz combines an essential Basqueness with a treatment inspired by the very best of French and Mediterranean cuisine. Everything is delicious, from a typical fish soup to the sort of thing not even dreamed of elsewhere, such as a grapefruit, spider crab and trout roe jelly with potato and olive oil cream. For a real gastronomic experience, order the €73 *menú de degustación*, a once-in-a-lifetime seven-course sonata of a meal.

€€ **Sansonategi**, Bº Martindegi s/n, **T** 943-553260. One of the few cider-houses to be open for meals all-year-round. Rates about midway on the authentic scale, and offers the traditional *menú sidrería* for €24, as well as good à la carte choices.

# West of San Sebastián

### Getaria and around

€€ **Asador Mayflower**, C Katrapona 4, Getaria, **T** 943-140658. One of a number of *asadors* in this attractive harbour town, with an excellent *menú del día*. Grilled sardines are a tasty speciality.

€€ **Kulixka**, C Bixkonde 1, Zarautz, **T** 943-831300. Welcoming waterfront restaurant with an unbeatable view of the beach. Good seafood as you'd expect, and a decent *menú del día* for €8.

€ **Mitate**, Berostigalle 13, Zarautz. A bizarre little *pintxo* bar in the old town, where locals gather to discuss football.

€ **Politena**, Kale Nagusia 9, Getaria, **T** 943-140113. A bar fairly oriented towards weekend visitors from Bilbao and San Sebastián. A very enticing selection of *pintxos*, and a €12.50 'weekend' *menú* which isn't bad either.

€ **Txalupa**, C Herrerieta 1, Getaria, **T** 943-140592. A great, hospitable bar to buy or taste the local fish and *txakolí*, and which offers *pintxos* as well as *cazuelitas*, small portions of bubbling stews or seafood in sauce.

# East of San Sebastián

## Hondarribia and around

€€€ **Sebastián**, Calle Mayor 9, Hondarribia, **T** 944-3640167.
Set in a dingy old grocery packed with interesting aromas, the food
exceeds the humble décor. Allegedly one of the best restaurants in
Euskadi, there's a good value *menú de degustación* for €38.

€€ **Medievo**, Plaza Guipúzcoa 8, Hondarribia, **T** 943-644509.  An
intriguing restaurant decorated in 21st-century medieval style. As
debatable as it sounds, it works, as does the imaginatively prepared food. Try the venison with prunes. There's a €9 *menú del día*.

€ **Bar Itxaropena**, C San Pedro 67, Hondarribia, **T** 943-641197.
Good bar in the new town offering a variety of cheap foodstuffs
and some good company at weekends.

# Vitoria/Gasteiz

As ever, the old town is good for bars, which are nearly all
clustered along Calle Cuchillería. Calle Eduardo Dato and the
streets crossing it are excellent for the early evening *pintxo* trail.

## Casco Medieval

€€€ **Arkupe**, C Mateo Moraza 13, **T** 945-230080.  A quality
restaurant serving imaginative dishes, such as a tasty squid 'n' potato
pie and inspiring salads. There's a *menú degustación* for €27.35.

€€ **Asador Matxete**, Plaza Machete 4, **T** 945-131821.  A stylish
modern restaurant harmoniously inserted into this pretty plaza
above *Los Arquillos*. Specialises in meat expertly grilled over coals.

€ **Bar El 7**, C Cuhillería 7, **T** 945-272298.  An excellent bar at the head of the Casco Medieval's liveliest street. Its big range of *bocadillos* keeps students and all-comers happy. Order a half if you're not starving; they make 'em pretty large.

€ **Cafeteria Marañon**, Plaza de la Virgen Blanca.  In the heart of Vitoria, this former ironmongers is not to be sneered at if you're on the prowl for a morning coffee and croissant.

€ **Hala Bedi**, C Cuchillería 98, **T** 945-260411.  A late-opening Basque bar with a cheerful atmosphere. Out of a tiny kitchen come crépes with a massive variety of sweet and savoury fillings.

€ **Korrokon**, C Cuchillería 9.  Tasty cheap food can be had here *al fresco* courtesy of a good range of simple *raciones*. The *mejillones* (mussels) in spicy tomato sauce are particularly good.

€ **Restaurante Zabala**, C Mateo Moraza 9, **T** 945-230099.  Although you wouldn't know it from the basic décor, this is a very well-regarded local restaurant. The dishes on offer, without being spectacular, are solid Basque and Rioja choices, and are priced fairly.

€ **Sherezade**, C Correría 42, **T** 945-255868.  A relaxed café, well frequented by students, and serving up good coffee and a range of *infusiones* (herb and fruit teas).

---

### New town

€€€ **Dos Hermanas**, C Madre Vedruna 10, **T** 945-132934.  One of Vitoria's oldest restaurants, but not the place to come for *nouvelle cuisine*, with generous, hearty and delicious traditional dishes

€€€ **Ikea**, Portal de Castilla 27, **T** 943-144747.  Lovers of homely Swedish furniture will be disappointed to discover that this is in fact one of Vitoria's best restaurants. Mainly French in style, with a few traditional Basque dishes on the agenda. There's a *menú de degustación* for €48, although ordering *à la carte* needn't cost much more.

€€ **Antiguo Felipe**, C Fueros 2, **T** 945-261808. A wooden basement restaurant in an old stone building. Easygoing atmosphere and a good line in fish for around €11 a main.

€€ **Baztertxo**, Plaza de España 14. A fine bar with some great wines by the glass and top-notch *jamón*. Although service can be beneath the dignity of the staff, it's a good choice nonetheless.

€€ **Eli Rekondo**, C Prado 28, **T** 945-282584. Characterful, and fairly intimate restaurant near Plaza de la Virgen Blanca. €33 *menú*.

€€ **Izago**, Tomás de Zumárraga 2, **T** 945-138200. Excellent eating is to be had in this fairly formal restaurant in a smart stone building. The focus is seafood, but there's plenty of other specialities – duck's liver on stuffed pig's ear, and some sinful desserts.

€€ **Restaurante Urdiña**, C San Antonio 22, **T** 945-233242. Despite the unattractive interior, there's some good nosh to be had. The emphasis is on simple traditional dishes done well. There's a *menú del día* for €9, and a *menú del degustación* at a more hefty €22.50.

€€ **Soka Tira**, C Las Trianas 15, **T** 945-140440. A fun place to eat and drink, this *sagardotegi* (cider house) offers the *menú sidrería* (see p) and plenty of cider vats to practice your decanting skills.

€ **El Jardín de América**, C Amárica 3, **T** 945-135217. Set on a square just off Calle Florida, you can sit outside and pick from a range of carefully prepared dishes in the €5-10 range. Good value.

€ **Restaurante Vegeteriano**, C Pedro Orbea 8,**T** 945-288701. Not the most inspiring of names, but a decent if simple meat-free lunchtime option which does a *menú* for €7.25.

€ **Café Jai Alai**, C Fueros 9, **T** 945-278037. There's a smartish after-work *pintxo* and cigar scene in this elegantly decorated bar.

€ **Café Los Angeles**, Plaza de Santo Domingo, **T** 945-144483. Bright and breezy modern two-level café which does a good line in fresh orange juice in the mornings, and stronger stuff after work.

€ **Café Moderno**, Plaza España 4, **T** 945-234448. Sunseekers should head here in the afternoon – the terrace in the postcardy arched square is perfectly placed for maximum rays.

€ **Cuatro Azules Florida**, Parque de la Florida, **T** 945-148848. One of Vitoria's best spots, with lots of tables amid the trees of this peaceful park. Regular games of boules take place nearby.

€ **Restaurante JG**, C Eduardo Dato 27, **T** 945-231132. Another excellent option for *pintxos* on this pedestrian street – the range of *croquetas* come highly recommended. More substantial eating is also good value in the *comedor*.

€ **Saburdi**, C Eduardo Dato 32, **T** 945-147016. Well worth popping in for the excellent fare atop the bar in this friendly local.

€ **Taberna**, C San Prudencio 21, **T** 945-231004. Simple dynamics: long bar, tables in the sun, big screen showing sport or films, beer, wine and pintxos.

# Alava/Araba

## Salvatierra

€€ **Merino**, Plaza de San Juan 3, Salvatierra, **T** 945-300052.
A sombre but reasonable bar/restaurant; the best option in town.

€ **Jose Mari**, C Mayor 73, Salvatierra, **T** 945-300042. The restaurant
does a evening *menú* for €8.10; smiles, apparently, cost extra.

# La Rioja Alavesa

€€ **Castillo El Collado**, Paseo El Collado 1, Laguardia,
**T** 945-621200.  There's an excellent, well-priced restaurant in this
beautiful fortified hotel at the northern end of Laguardia.

€€ **El Bodegón**, Travesía Santa Engracia 3, Laguardia,
**T** 945-600793.  Tucked away in the middle of old Laguardia is this
cosy restaurant, with a €11 *menú del dia* focusing on the hearty
staples of the region, such as *pochas* (beans), or *patatas con chorizo*.

€€ **Hotel Antigua Bodega de Don Cosme Palacio**, Carretera
Elciego s/n, Laguardia, **T** 945-621195.  This hotel restaurant makes
an effort to showcase local cuisine, with a couple of challenging *menús*
as well as *à la carte* dishes. Closed Sunday evenings and Mondays.

€€ **Marixa**, C Sancho Abarca s/n, Laguardia, **T** 945-600165.
In the Hotel Marixa, this is a good place to eat. The dining room
boasts great views over the vine-covered plains below and has a
range of local specialities with formally correct Spanish service.
The wine list ain't bad either.

€€ **Mesón La Cueva**, Concepción 15, Oyon, **T** 945-601022.
If you're visiting wineries over this way, a hearty lunch here is in
order. This dark and gloomy restaurant specializes in well-executed
Riojan cuisine, and cooks some decent vegetarian dishes too,
which is a nice change. *Menú* for €14.50.

€ **Biazteri**, C Berberana 2, Laguardia, **T** 945-600026. One of the
cheaper places in Laguardia, this down-to-earth bar does some
fine *platos combinados*, with very tranquil outside seating.

Distinction between different types of hostelry is never clear in Spain. What starts the day as a coffee 'n' croissant stop for office workers might end it with the lights fading, the music pumping and frighteningly large gin and tonics being poured after dark. The listings in this section are generally places that open late, close late, and don't serve food. Many bars only open at the weekend; Basques aren't big midweek revellers. All three cities have plenty of barlife; Bilbao inevitably offers more options, although in summer San Sebastián gives it a run for its money. The clubbing scene in the Basque lands isn't great. Bona fide clubs (*discotecas*) are fairly few in number, and many are solely devoted to the Spanish Top Four. San Sebastián has a number of high-profile discotecas which complement its beachside scene, but more interesting venues are to be found in Bilbao. Many clubs don't open their doors until after midnight, and keep things going until well after dawn. Few are open during the week.

# Bilbao/Bilbo

## Bars

**Bilbo Rock**, Muelle de la Merced s/n, **T** 944-151306.
Map 2 E12, p249  Atmospheric venue in a converted church, now a temple of live rock. Bands play most nights at 2100 or 2200.

**Bizitza**, C Torre 1. Map 1, E2, p247  Very chilled predominantly gay bar with a Basque political slant. Frequent cultural events.

**Braveheart**, C Hurtado de Amézaga 22. Map 2, E11, p249  Take yourself for a wee swallie at this friendly place. The theme continues behind the bar, where there's a good range of malt whisky.

**Cómic's**, C Principe 3. Map 2, B11, p249  A cheery place with some interesting music and a very late last-drinks call at weekends.

**Compañia del Ron**, C Máximo Aguirre 23. Map 2, F7, p249  Friends of Ronald will be happy, with over 100 rums at the bar staff's disposal. A good early-evening spot, despite the chain-pub feel.

**Consorcio**, C Barrencalle Barrena 10, **T** 944-169904. Map 1, E2, p247  After getting past the imposing front wall you'll find a decent pre-club bar which occasionally has events midweek too.

**Covent Garden**, C Doctor Areilza 28. Map 2, H6, p248  A dark wooden corridor of a pub, with some quirky decoration, including a model train which does laps of the place above head height.

**Gales**, C Licenciado Poza 49. Map 2, G6, p248  The name means Wales in Spanish, but this bar is definitely inspired from the other side of the Atlantic; kitted out with Aztec totems and motifs.

**K2**, C Somera 10. *Map 1, E4, p247* One of the last to shut in the Casco on weeknights, this is quite a big bar with seating, a varied set of folk and exhibitions on the walls.

**Luz Gas**, C Pelota 6, **T** 944-790823. *Map 1, F2, p247* A beautiful mood bar with an Oriental touch. Sophisticated but friendly, and you can challenge all-comers to chess or Connect-4.

**Mitote**, Belostikale. From some angles this bar looks like a British bed 'n' breakfast, while other views take in bizarre Botero frescoes. Quiet weeknights, at weekends it's a cheerfully packed bar unwinding to unchallenging music. Try to visit a toilet before showing up.

**Scuba Duba**, C Principe 1. *Map 2, B11, p249* Another late-opener on this tiny street. Popular music from Spain and the USA.

**Terranova**, C Licenciado Poza 6 (corner of C Elkano). *Map 2, F9, p249* A bar with a good attitude and Friday 'chill-out' music sessions.

**The Dubliners**, Plaza Moyúa. *Map 2, E7, p249* "You can't go out in Dublin any more, there's too many Irish pubs". The craze has well and truly hit Bilbao; this is the best known. Good after-work atmosphere, and a range of events through the week.

**Twiggy**, Alameda de Urquijo 35. *Map 2, F9, p249* Psychedelic colours and a 60s feel characterize this bar in one of the busiest weekend hubs.

**Zulo**, Barrenkale 22. *Map 1, E3, p247* A tiny nationalist bar with plenty of plastic fruit and a welcoming set who definitely don't follow the Bill Clinton line on non-inhalation. The name means 'hole' in Euskara.

## Clubs

**Caché Latino**, C Ripa 3. *Map 2, C12, p249* This riverside bar is a sweaty den of merengue and salsa with a slightly volatile atmosphere but pretty authentic music. Watch your possessions closely.

**Café Indie**, C Doctor Areilza 34. *Map 2, H6, p248* Trendier and sleeker than the name might suggest. Sofas downstairs, and a bar and dancefloor upstairs. At weekends this makes some of the other clubs look empty, with both music and crowd that are suspiciously on the mainstream side of indie. British retro gets some play too.

**Congreso**, Muelle de Uribitarte 4. *Map 2, B10, p249* A classic *bakalao* and house venue, hardly cutting edge but a mainstay of the Bilbao scene. Doesn't really get into its stride until four or so in the morning. Mixed crowd. Open Friday and Saturday nights.

**Conjunto Vacío**, C Muelle de la Merced 4. *Map 2, E12, p249* Empty by name and packed by nature, at least from about 0200 on Fridays and Saturday. The music is fairly light bakalao, the crowd mixed and good-looking, the drinks horrendously expensive, but the entry free.

**Cotton Club**, C Gregorio de la Revilla 25. *Map 2, H7, p249* Live music venue with a relaxed atmosphere and lined with characterful trappings from the world of showbiz. Music ranges from rock to jazz.

**Distrito 9**, Alameda Rekalde 18. *Map 2, D7, p249* Still probably the best spot in Bilbao for house music. Goes very late and is quite a dressy scene. Drag shows and a €10 cover.

**★ Nationalist bars**

**Best**

- Zulo, Casco Viejo, Bilbao, p178.
- Arrauna, Parte Vieja, San Sebastián, p182.
- Jaunak, Casco Viejo, Bilbao, p151.
- Arrana, Gernika, p179.
- Almost any bar in Ondarroa… the town buzzes with Basqueness, p181.

**Kafe Antzokia**, C San Vicente 2, **T** 944-244625,www.kafeantzokia. com  *Map 2, C10, p249*  An ex-cinema fast becoming a Bilbao icon, this is a live venue for anything from death metal to Euskara poetry, and features two spacious floors with bars which go late and loud at weekends.

**La Lola**, C Bailén 10.  €5 at the door.  *Map 2, E12, p249*  Decorated in industrial style with sheet-metal and graffiti, this is a good Saturday night club that varies in character from fairly cheesy dance to pretty heavy garage. Open until 0600, and then runs as a Sunday day club from 2330.

**New Garden**, C Lehendakari Aguirre 13, **T** 944-760056. *Map 2, E1, p248*  Next to the Casa Vasca restaurant, this place has a double identity. During the week it features some fairly nostalgic music with older couples dancing. At weekends it fills with students and the pop goes on late.

**Zodiakos**, C Euskal Herria s/n (corner of Telletxe), **T** 944-604059. This squiggly bar in the heart of Getxo is one of the area's best, with a terrace, pintxos, and service with a smile. Underneath is *Alai*, a weekend discoteca.

*Bars and clubs*

# Inland

## Bars

**Arrana**, C Juan Calzada 6, Gernika.  A vibrant Basque bar with a lively young crowd spilling outside at weekends.

**Bar Irritz**, Calle Zaharri, Oñati.  A late-opening weekend bar on Oñati's main street. Popular techno and a friendly scene.

**Lezika**, Cuevas de Santamamiñe, Kortezubi, Gernika.  The whole of Vizcaya seems to descend on the beer garden here at weekends with kids and dogs in tow; the restaurant is worthwhile, and better value than the meagre *raciones* on offer at the bar.

**Metropol**, Cnr C Unamuno and Iparragirre, Gernika.  A cavernous and comradely bar, open later than anywhere and then some.

**Parra Taberna**, Elorrio.  A peaceful bar with tables on the main square and a beautiful glass and stone interior.

**Sakris**  In Markina's old town back streets, this tiny bar, in a 17th-century palace, is one of the more atmospheric choices in relaxed Markina.

# The Basque Coastline

## Bars

**Ku-Kua**, Kanttoipe, Ondarroa.  A very lively bar that gets very full and goes on very late.

**La Leñera**.  A friendly bar in Mundaka's tiny back streets. No *pintxos* but plenty of seats.

**Nasa Kalea**, in Ondarroa, is well-stocked with bars, many of which are temples to Basque rock, which is heavily identified with the independence movement. Two worth dropping in on are Apallu, at number 30, and Sansonategi.

**Talako**, Leikeitio, above the *fisherman's co-operative*.   A great spot for one of Lekeitio's rainy days, with a pool table, board games, and a 180º view of the harbour, town and beaches.

**The Music School**, Ondarroa.  On the corner of Iñaki Deunaren and Sabino Arana (Arana'tar Sabin)  There is often live Basque alternative rock on Friday or Saturday nights – it's usually free and worth a look, especially if you're a fan of Spanish music as a whole.

# San Sebastián/Donostia

## Bars

**Altxerri Bar**, C Reina Regenta 2.  *Map 4, B5, p252*  An atmospheric cellar bar which regularly showcases live jazz and other acts. Draws an interesting crowd and is worthwhile even if there's nothing on.

**Arkaitzpe**, C Mayor 14, **T** 943-421867.  *Map 4, B3, p252*  A good bar, modern, blue, and relaxed. Later at night the tables disappear and the dancing starts.

**Arrauna**, C Angel 2.  *Map 4, B3, p252*  In a quiet corner of the Parte Vieja, this is a committedly leftist Basque bar and a solid place to hole up when the weather closes in.

**Bar Eiger**, C General Jauregi 4.   *Map 4, A4, p252*   A warm, very happy little bar near the river.

**Bar El Cine**, C San Bartolomé 21, **T** 943-460783.
*Map 4, F3, p253*   Long-standing student favourite in this busy zone. A massive complex with loud, cheesy music and several bars. Open until dawn at weekends.

**Bar Ondarra**, Av de la Zurriola 16.   *Map 4, A7, p252*   Opposite the Kursaal exhibition centre in Gros, this is a decent bar with a small street level and an underground den featuring regular live jazz and soul.

**Bideluze**, Plaza Guipúzcoa 14.   *Map 4, C5, p252*   Two floors of eccentric furniture on the south side of Plaza Guipúzcoa, serving food.

**El Ensanche**, C San Vicente.   *Map 4, A4, p252*   Small but characterful *perro* and *porro* sort of Basque bar.

**El Nido**, C Larramendi 13.   *Map 4, F5, p252*   A sizeable pub which fills after work and doesn't empty again until late. Friendly crowd and board games.

**Etxekalte**, C Mari 11.   *Map 4, B3, p252*   On the harbour side of the old town, this is a popular and atmospheric place to hang out on a Saturday night. The music played is mostly jazz.

**Garagar**, Alameda del Boulevard 22, **T** 943-422840.   *Map 4, B4, p252*   Slightly overpriced pub at the edge of the Parte Vieja with some comfy booths. Keeps 'em pouring until 0200 most nights (0400 at weekends), and it's much more relaxing than some of the other tourist-oriented late-openers. DJ upstairs at weekends.

**Museo del Whisky**, Alameda del Boulevard, **T** 943-426478, museo@telefonica.net  *Map 4, C4, p252*  As good as its name, with over 3,000 different bottles on site. It's a very relaxing place to sit back with a single malt, and there's a piano bar downstairs. The superb range of drams doesn't come cheap, however.

**Soma 107**, C Larramendi 4, **T** 943-468810.  *Map 4, F5, p252*  Every facet of this remarkable bar is devoted to making the smoking of *porros* as chilled as possible. It's almost a dope centre rather than a mere bar, with internet, books, food, and two levels of seating sensitively decorated with cool murals, graffiti and paintings.

## Clubs

**Bataplán**, Playa de la Concha s/n, **T** 943-460439.  *Map 4, F2, p252*  San Sebastián's most famous discoteca, right on La Concha beach. Open Thursday-Saturday for a smart young crowd from midnight onwards. The music is pretty much what you'd expect for a resort club; mostly club anthems and pop crowd-pleasers. Rises to prominence during the film festival when it hosts various after-parties. €12-15 entry.

**Discobolo**, Boulevard 27.  *Map 4, C4, p252*  A tacky option just outside Parte Vieja. Far from cutting edge, but cheerful atmosphere.

**Kandela**, C Escolta Real 20, Antiguo.  This bar in the suburb of Antiguo usually features live bands from Thursday to Sunday. It ranges from rock to pop and usually kicks off at about 2300. The €6 entry includes a drink.

**Komplot**, C Pedro Egaña 5, **T** 943-472109.  *Map 4, C5, p252*  Small and *à la mode* club featuring probably the best house music in San Sebastián. Just next to the Euskotren station.

**Ku**, Monte Igueldo s/n.  Atop the Igueldo hill at the end of Ondarreta beach is one of the city's more glamorous discos, with a smart mixed crowd. Usually goes on later than anywhere.

**La Kabutzia**, Paseo de la Concha s/n, **T** 943-429785.  *Map 4, C3, p252* Situated in the shiplike *Real Club Naútico* on the beach, this is a well-situated club with a young crowd.

**Rotonda**, Playa de la Concha 6, **T** 943-429095.  *Map 4, F1, p252* Another club on La Concha beach,  open very late weekend nights. The music on offer varies, but usually hovers around popular dance, with some salsa and reggae thrown in as required.

# Vitoria/Gasteiz

### Bars

There are quite a few bars on Zapatería, Correría and around Plaza de la Burullería, mostly weekend only, and plenty of bars around San Francisco and Fueros.

**Bar El 7**, C Cuhillería 7, **T** 945-272298.  An excellent bar at the head of the Casco Medieval's liveliest street. Its big range of *bocadillos* keeps students and all-comers happy. Order a half if you're not starving; they make 'em pretty large.

**Bar Rio**, C Eduardo Dato 20, **T** 945-230067.  A decent café with outdoor tables by day, and one of the last bars to shut at night, when it caters to a good-natured gay/straight crowd. Original live music on Thursday nights.

**Cruz Blanco**, C San Prudencio 26.   This cavernous *cervecería* is a popular evening drinking spot with several outdoor tables and decent-sized *cañas*. Handy for the cinema and theatre.

**Hala Bedi**, C Cuchillería 98, **T** 945-260411.   A late-opening Basque bar with a cheerful atmosphere, serving delicious crepes.

## Clubs

**Aural**, C Paseo de la Senda 2, **T** 945-147400.   A fairly refined club as these things go, with a very trendy interior and chart hits alongside a fair whack of nostalgia. A more mature crowd than many.

**Cairo Stereo Club**, C Aldabe 9.   Excellent Vitorian club with some excellent and innovative DJs and a mixed crowd. During the week they often show cult movies or hold theme parties.

**Gallery**, Plaza San Antón 4, **T** 945-250502.   A young and lively set of punters make this a good place to come for *bacalao* and house.

**Pravda**, C Guerrillero Fernández de Leceta 7.   Grungy small underground venue with a young druggy crowd. Music tends towards the trance-y. Busiest night is Saturday.

**Swing**, C Bastiturri 1, **T** 945-281372.   A reasonable club that doesn't veer much from a comfortable pop and techno line. Mixed crowd with a strong lesbian scene.

**Tapioca**, C Sancho El Sabio 22, **T** 945-247471.   A relaxed and fairly funky club with music from soul through to soft house. Open until 0500 at weekends. Interesting decoration includes exhibitions by young local artists.

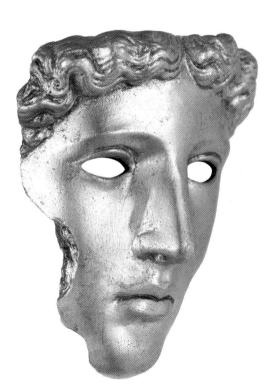

# Cinema

Nearly all foreign films shown in the Basque Country are dubbed. There's significant resistance in Spain to subtitles, which springs not least from the dubbers themselves, who have a relatively lucrative career laid out if one of the actors whose lines they speak makes it big in Hollywood. If your Spanish is so-so, it's usually easier to understand Spanish films than dubbed ones; being able to read the lips is a big help. Nearly all sessions are around the €5 mark, sometimes discounted for earlier sessions or quieter nights. Typical session times would be 1700, 2000 and 2230.

## Bilbao

**Cines Avenida**, C Lehendakari Aguirre 18, **T** 944-757796.  *Metro: Deusto.*  Map 2, D1, p248  In Deusto, this is one of the better cinemas around, which tends to show a few lower profile releases and artier films, as well as some Basque pictures.

**Cinema Mikeldi**, Alameda Urquijo 66, **T** 944-411728.  *Metro: Indautxu.*  Map 2, G7, p249  A smallish but convenient cinema on Plaza Indautxu, showing a handful of major releases.

**Cines Multis**, C José María Escuza 13.  *Metro: San Mamés.*  Map 2, H5, p248  This complex shows more interesting releases than some, and also has more Spanish-language pictures.

**Ideal Cinema**, C Egaña 1, **T** 944-210561.  *Metro: Indautxu.*  Map 2, G10, p249  Large complex near Plaza Zabalburu showing mostly big releases, but occasionally dedicated to short topical festivals.

**Lauren Getxo Zinemak**, Muelle Arriluce s/n.  *Metro: Neguri.*  A big complex on the pier in Getxo with a dozen screens showing mostly no-brainers.

## San Sebastián

**Antzoki Zaharra**, C Mayor 3, **T** 943-426112. *Map 4, B3, p252*
In the Parte Vieja, this auditorium showcases offbeat cinema and
theatre.

**Cines Ilunbe**, Paseo Miramón 2. In the complex around the
bullring, this is a large and modern centre showing big-budget
flicks to a youngish crowd.

**Cines Principe**, C San Juan 8-12, San Sebastián. *Map 4, A4, p252*
A large, central cinema opposite the San Telmo museum.

**Cines Trueba**, Plaza Esnaola s/n, Gros. *Map 4, B7, p252* One of
the only moviehouses in the Basque country to show regular
*versión original* English language films.

## Vitoria

**Cines Florida**, C San Prudencio 24. Very large and central
Vitorian cinema with a variety of films on offer.

**Cines Guridi**, C San Prudencio 6. Between them, this and the
allied Florida a couple of blocks away cover plenty of bases.

**Cines Mikeldi**, Portal de Villareal 44. A fairly standard cinematic
experience.

# Comedy

Spanish comedy isn't as high-profile an art as in the UK, for example. It's an unusual experience, usually presented as a restaurant or
café cabaret-style performance.

**La Tramoya**, C Elkano 26, Bilbao, **T** 944-217132. Bilbao's best known venue for comedy; a somewhat kitsch restaurant with decent if uninspired cuisine and comedy shows on Friday and Saturday nights. Booking essential.

## Dance

Euskadi is a great place for contemporary dance; there's nearly always something interesting going on. Local troupes adapt traditional Basque dances, while styles from further afield such as *flamenco* can also be seen. There are few dedicated dance venues but most of the establishments listed under 'theatre' devote a good portion of their programming to this muse. Ballet isn't the big thing in these parts; check the Arriaga in Bilbao or the Kursaal in San Sebastián for any that might be on.

**La Fundición**, C Francisco Macía 1, **T** 944-753327. *Metro: Deusto. Map 2, D2, p247* Just across the Deusto bridge, this small set-up puts on much fascinating dance from around the globe, as well as some excellent theatre from small companies.

## Music

Opera and classical performances are alive and kicking in all three of the Basque cities, boosted by the opening of the Kursaal and the Euskalduna. Fiestas aside, there isn't a huge scene in popular live music, but there are several good venues in each place.

The notable exception is Basque rock, whose real home is in the smaller towns of Euskadi; leave the cities and it's guaranteed that, wherever the pro-independence posters are concentrated, somewhere nearby there'll be a local band giving out some large, heavy and anthemic songs of freedom.

**Altxerri Bar**, C Reina Regenta 2.  *Map 4, B5, p252*  An atmospheric cellar bar which regularly showcases live jazz and other acts. Draws an interesting crowd and is worthwhile even if there's nothing on.

**Be Bop Bar**, Paseo de Salamanca 3.  Corner of General Echagüe. *Map 4, B5, p252*  A quiet bar that features regular live jazz.

**Cotton Club**, C Gregorio de la Revilla 25.  *Metro: Indautxu. Map 2, H7, p249*  Live music venue with a relaxed atmosphere and lined with characterful trappings from the world of showbiz. Music ranges from rock to jazz.

**Kafe Antzokia**, C San Vicente 2, **T** 944-244625.  *Metro: Abando. Map 2, C10, p249*  An ex-cinema fast becoming a Bilbao icon, this is a live venue for anything from death metal to Euskara poetry, and features two spacious floors with, late and loud, weekends bars.

**Kandela**, C Escolta Real 20, Antiguo.  This bar in the suburb of Antiguo usually features live bands from Thurday to Sunday. It ranges from rock to pop and usually kicks off at about 2300. The €6 entry includes a drink.

**Palacio Euskalduna**, C Abandoibarra 4, **T** 944-310310.  *Euskotren: Abandoibarra; Metro: San Mamés.  Map 2, F3, p248*  Top-quality classical performances from the symphonic orchestras of Bilbao and Euskadi, as well as high-profile Spanish and international artists.

**Teatro Arriaga**, see Theatre, p193.  Regular  opera.

---

### San Sebastián

**Kursaal auditorium**, Av Zurriola 1, San Sebastián, **T** 943-003000. *Map 4, A6, p252*  San Sebastián's new architectural pride hosts world-class classical concerts and opera.

*Some love it, some hate it. San Sebastián's new Kursaal shines in the setting sun. Venue for concerts and theatre, it also hosts the International Film Festival, when celebrities can be spotted sunning themselves like mermaids on the rocks.*

## Vitoria

**Musika Eskola**, Ondarroa.  The music school, on the corner of Iñaki Deunaren and Sabino Arana (Arana'tar).

**Sabin** often has live Basque alternative rock on Friday or Saturday nights – it's usually free and definitely worth a look, especially if you're not a fan of Spanish music as a whole.

**Teatro Antzokia**, see Theatre, p194. Regular concerts and opera.

# Theatre

After a fallow period during Franco's lengthy tenure, professional theatre in the Basque Country has now taken its rightful place as a vehicle of Basque expression. Performances are frequently one-offs or on very short runs but typically are energetic, imaginative and avant-garde. A huge range of shows are presented even in the larger theatres; there's a seriously exploratory spirit that is very invigorating, even if it occasionally strays into the politically naïve.

### Bilbao

**Teatro Arriaga**, Plaza Arriaga 1, **T** 944-792036. *Metro: Abando/Casco Viejo.  Map 2, D12, p248*  Bilbao's highest profile theatre is picturesquely set on the river by the Casco Viejo. It's a plush treat of a theatre in late-19th century style, but the work it presents can be very innovative. The better seats go for €25 and above, but there are often decent pews available for as little as €4-5. Box-office is open business hours.

**Teatro Ayala**, C Manuel Allende 18, **T** 944-212260. *Metro: Indautxu.  Map 2, H7, p248*  Bilbao's second major theatre, with slightly more conservative programming than the Arriaga.

Teatro Barakaldo, C Juán Sebastián Elkano 4, **T** 944-780600. *Metro: Barakaldo.*  In the barrio of Barakaldo, this theatre presents a very diverse progamme of local and touring theatre, music and dance

### San Sebastián

**Antzoki Zaharra**, C Mayor 3, San Sebastián, **T** 943-426112.  *Map 4, B3, 0p252*  This auditorium showcases offbeat cinema and theatre.

### Vitoria

**Teatro Antzokia**, C San Prudencio 29, Vitoria, **T** 945-161045. Vitoria's principal theatre, with blink or you'll miss it programming of a good variety of shows.

If the sun rises in the east, it's a sure sign that there's a festival somewhere in Euskadi that day. From tragic to bizarre, from solemn to slapstick, even the smallest village has its day (or week); many have several. The majority of the fiestas are traditional and have some sort of religious basis, in many cases pre-dating Christianity. Fiestas in larger towns will usually feature corridas or other bull-sports, as well as live music, markets, and street performances. There's usually a procession (or six): even the more comedic ones usually have a symbolic significance; it's worth asking around to find the meaning behind the figures. Whatever the occasion, whatever the weather, young and old will descend on the town from all around, pacing the streets, slurping kalimotxo (red wine mixed with Coke; not as bad as it sounds, at least until the next morning), and taking riotous advantage of the bars, which usually stay open all night.

There are also more modern festivals, particularly music and cinema based. It's difficult to find accommodation during fiestas if you haven't booked; if worst comes to worst lock your bags in the bus or train station and make a night of it; you'll be in good company. This is far from a complete listing of Euskadi's festivals but includes the major ones. The annual fiesta in a tiny village, if you stumble across it, can be just as boisterous, quirky, and kicking as the best-organized Bilbao showpiece.

## January
**Tamborrada** (19th-20th), San Sebastián. The day of the 'pincushion saint' is celebrated with a deafening parade of drummers through the streets from midnight on the 19th. It's said that the custom originated around the town well, when a group of local lasses started banging on the buckets they were waiting to fill. Many of the drummers dress as chefs; as members of the gastronomic societies of the city, they adjourn to the kitchen after the parade to prepare the mother of all midnight feasts.
**San Anastasio** (22nd), Oyon (Alava). This Riojan town celebrates this fiesta by parading a figure named Katxi through the streets.

## February
**Carnaval** usually kicks off on the Saturday before Ash Wednesday, continuing through to Shrove Tuesday, which is 47 days before Easter Sunday (Sundays don't count in the 40-day fast). There are celebrations everywhere; San Sebastián starts early and is lively for the whole period, as are Bilbao, Vitoria and Tolosa, where the Sunday festivities are considered the liveliest in Euskadi.
More traditional carnivals can be seen in smaller towns such as Salvatierra and Zalduondo in Alava, and Markina in Vizcaya.

## March/April
**Semana Santa** (Easter week) sees much activity throughout the regon. Bilbao marks the occasion with a number of serious hooded

processions accompanied by mournful drums and cornets, from Passion Friday onwards. One of the best known Easter events is in the western Vizcayan town of Balmaseda where the stations of the Cross are re-enacted by residents. The moving performance is taken very seriously; the person who is to play Christ begins to study the role three years in advance. Hondarribia also puts on a similar play. In the village of Salinas de Añana, Alava, Judas is put on trial, convicted and then burned; the poor guy must be wondering when he's going to get an even break. First Sunday after Easter sees an **encierro** (running of bulls) on the beach in the town of Zumaia to celebrate the day of San Telmo. **San Prudencio's day** (28th) is celebrated throughout Alava with tamborradas, an enactment of his life is given in Vitoria the night before.

## May

**Fantasy Cinema festival** (1st-5th) in Bilbao, with short films, make-up courses, exhibitions, and discussions. For **Pentecost** weekend (seven weeks after Easter), the town of Bergara celebrates its fiesta with bull-sports, concerts, and a corrida. **Corpus Christi** (Thursday after Trinity Sunday, eight weeks after Easter). Festivities in many towns, notably Oñati (Guipúzcoa), where traditional religious Basque dances are performed, especially the espata dantza, sword dance. **Maritime fair** (29nd-31st) in Bermeo.

## June

**Getxo blues festival** (second week) in the Plaza Santa Eugenia. A lively fiesta in the Guipúzcoan town of Segura. Mid-June. **San Juan** (24th) has his day in the sun in many places, notably Tolosa and Laguardia. The night before, bonfires are lit in many villages, echoing pre-Christian summer solstice celebrations. In San Sebastián, the **Semana Gastronómica** (last week) is a treat for the taste buds. **San Pedro** (29th) steps up, celebrated particularly in Lekeitio, where the tricky kaxarranka is danced on top of a chest hoisted to shoulder height and carried around town.

## July

**Getxo jazz festival** (first week). **Encierro** in Zumaia (first week).
**Virgen del Carmen** (16th) sees effigies of the Lady carried out to
sea in a picturesque procession of fishing boats, particularly at
Plentzia and Santurtzi on either side of the Bilbao estuary.
**International Jazz Festival** (third week) in Vitoria.
**International Jazz Festival** (second fortnight) in San Sebastián.
**La Magdalena** (22nd) series of nautical events and races in and
around Bermeo. **Santiago's day** (25th) is celebrated around the
traps but particularly in Vitoria as the **Día del Blusa** (blouse day)
when colour-co-ordinated kids patrol the streets. Hondarribia also
celebrates with a slightly bizarre procession of a box of documents
from the fishermen's guild to the local church. **International
Paella Competition** (25th) in Getxo. **Fiesta de San Pedro**
(29th) in Mundaka, with much traditional dancing. **San Ignacio's
day** (3rd) is celebrated in Loiola and Getxo.

## August

The major month for Basque festivals, you can spend nearly the
whole of August at the major fiestas of the three cities. **Fiesta de
la Virgen Blanca** (4th-9th) in Vitoria, the city's major knees-up
comes thoroughly recommended. Getaria celebrates the **Festival
of San Salvador** (7th). Every four years a re-enactment of the
landing of Elkano is staged (next one in 2003). **Festival of San
Nicolás** (12th) is celebrated in the picturesque old port of Getxo.
The **Aste Nagusia** (week before the 15th) or 'big week' kicks off in
San Sebastián with world-renowned fireworks exhibitions.

   The major fiestas of **Gernika** and **Markina** (15th-16th). Bilbao's
turn for a big week (Saturday after the 15th); a boisterous mixture
of everything; concerts, corridas, traditional Basque sports, and
serious drinking. San Sebastián tempts fate by commemorating
the **Great Fire of 1813** (31st) with a huge display of candles.

## September

**Euskal Jaiak** (first week), a celebration of Basque crafts, culture and food and another reason to stuff yourself in San Sebastián! **International folk festival** (first week), Getxo. **San Antolín** (4th), Lekeitio's seriously weird goose festival. **Fiesta of the Virgen de Guadalupe** (8th) in Hondarribia, commemorating her decisive intervention in a 1639 battle. **Euskal Jaiak** (9th) in Zarautz, a celebration of Basque crafts and food. **International Film Festival** (third week), San Sebastián. **San Miguel's day** (29th), is celebrated in Oñati and Markina with dancing and plenty of consumption of the beverage bearing his name.

## October

Parade and the **aurresku** (first Sunday), a traditional dance, in Elorrio. **Harvest time** in the Rioja Alavesa (first week), a happy season with much celebration. **Horror film festival**, (first and last week of November), San Sebastián.

## November

An **international theatre festival** in Vitoria lasts from October to December. **International Competition of Short Films and Documentaries** in Bilbao.

## December

**Advent**, Vitoria is known for its spectacular full-sized Nativity scene, with over 200 figures. On the weekend before Christmas, the character **Olentzero**, a charcoal seller, announces the approach of Christmas in Basque towns and villages. Townspeople of San Sebastián (24th) climb Monte Igueldo with an effigy of a **besugo** (sea bream), a fish that has fed the Basques well over the centuries. An open-air midnight mass (24th) is held by firelight in **Labastida** in the Rioja Alavesa.

Shopping

Whether it's some unusual Spanish fashion, a chorizo and a bottle of Rioja, or six cartons of Marlboro Lights to get through the month, you're bound to want to hit the shops at some stage. Bilbao is by far the best place to shop in the Basque region; San Sebastián and Vitoria have their share of stores, but there's a bigger range and more quirky options in the bigger city. Opening hours vary, but shops normally up shutters at 0930 or 1000, break for lunch at 1400, come back at 1700, and stay open until 2000 or 2030. Most shops are open at least on Saturday mornings, and many clothes shops are open all weekend. Spain isn't as cheap as it once was, and the advent of the Euro will undoubtedly further narrow the price gap. Clothes are by no means cheap in the Basque country, but there are a number of well-priced Spanish houses that don't have outlets elsewhere and are worth investigating. Wine is cheaper than in Britain, and spirits, extraordinarily so (although low taxes surely won't be in place long). Delicatessen goods such as ham, cheese and olive oil are also good purchases.

There are frequent markets across the region; most towns and villages have a weekly food and clothing market, while Bilbao has a small but quirky flea market in the Plaza Nueva on Sundays. These are the only places where bargaining goes on, but it's only on non-food items.

## Books

**Casa del Libro**, C Arka 11, Vitoria, **T** 945-158175. *Daily 0930-2030*. A comprehensive bookshop with plenty of English titles.

**Topbooks**, Gran Vía 22, Bilbao. *Map 2, D9, p248* One of the larger bookshops in town, with a fair selection of Spanish, Euskara, and English titles.

## Crafts

**Bilbo Carnaval**, Cnr Artekale and Tendería, Bilbao. *Map 1, E3, p247* A selection of dolls and costumes guaranteed to get you in that pre-Lent spirit.

**Gaston y Daniela**, Cnr C Correo and Cinturería, Bilbao. *Map 1, E3, p247* A beautifully painted building houses this venerable carpet and fabric shop in the heart of the Casco Viejo.

**Intermon**, Alameda Urquijo 11, Bilbao. *Map 2, E10, p249* An eclectic mix of handcrafts with the emphasis on fair trade. There are items from the everyday to the fanciful.

**Tentaciones**, C Buenos Aires 12, Bilbao. *Map 2, C11, p249* A selection of small gifts, paste jewellery and other curiosities.

**Txorrerri**, Artekale 25, Bilbao. *Map 1, E4, p247* A good little shop peddling homemade honey and other cottage products.

## Department stores

**Corte Inglés**, Gran Vía 7, Bilbao, C La Paz, Vitoria, **T** 944-253500/
5266333 *Mon-Sat until 2200. Map 2, D10, p248* The usual several
floors of everything.

## Fashion

**Adolfo Dominguez**, C Arias 16, Bilbao. *Map 2, F7, p249*
Selection of smartish casual to semi-formal men's vestments.
Fairly pricey and designer-ish in style.

**Amsterdam Plein**, C Askao 2/Plaza Nueva, Bilbao. *Map 1, C3,
p247* Individual clothing for the young alternative set.

**Bershka**, C Arias 17, Bilbao. *Map 2, F8, p249* A warehouse-sized
depository for some Britney-trendy clothes for teens and young
women.

**Falstaff**, C Colon de Larreátegui 29, Bilbao. *Map 2, D9,
p249* Despite the name, this punts out some pretty original
clothing for young-at- heart women.

**Kukuxumusu**, C Arias 27, Bilbao. *Map 2, F7, p249* A happy shop
with a range of cheerful Basque t-shirts in bright colours.

**Static**, C de la Torre s/n, Bilbao. *Map 1, E3, p247* Some very
happening streetwear from Necronomicon and other indie labels.

**Trantxo**, C Somera 8, Bilbao. *Map 1, E4, p247* Alternative fashion
on this alternative street.

**Wakalouka**, C Diputación 4, Bilbao. *Map 1, E9, p249* All your needs for the Basque surfing scene are catered for, as well as snow gear.

## Food and drink

**Arreser**, Gran Vía 24, Bilbao. *Map 2, D9, p249* A historic pastelería with an intriguing selection of cakes and sweeties.

**Chocolates de Mendaro**, C Licenciado Poza 14, Bilbao. *Map 2, F8, p249* A tiny shop selling boutique chocolates that are just too gorgeous to eat... maybe.

**Claudio**, C Esperanza 48, Bilbao. *Map 1, B1, p247* Respected shop dealing in cured pigs' legs. Try before you buy.

**Ibeas**, C Licenciado Poza 27, Bilbao. *Map 2, G7, p249* A classy shop with a range of good wines, spirits and gourmet deli products, as well as wrapped gifts and hampers.

**La Brecha**, Plaza de Bretxa, San Sebastián (see Sights, p90). *Map 4, B4, p252* Market complex in the old town.

**La Moderna**, C Astarloa 6, Bilbao. *Map 2, D9, p249* In a land of *jamón* and *chorizo*, a German deli of all things, doing a roaring trade too.

**Mercado de la Ribera**, C Ribera s/n, Bilbao (see p37). *Map 1, F3, p247* Three floors of market produce on the edge of the old town.

**Oka**, C Colon de Larreátegui 33 (Cnr C Marqués del Puerto), Bilbao. *Map 2, D8, p249* A small but excellent corner deli, particularly strong on cheese, but with some good jamones too.

## Music

**Frudisk**, C Miracruz 6, San Sebastián. *Map 4, C7, p252* A decent Gros music shop that also does internet access.

**Tipo**, C Somera 39, Bilbao. *Map 1, E4, p247* Decent record shop with a fair alternative section.

## Other

**Athletic Bilbao shop**, Alameda Rekalde 44, Bilbao. *Map 2, F8, p249* Your one-stop shop for all souvenirs relating to Los Leones. If it's not red and white, it's not on.

**Barandiaran**, C Navarra 1, Bilbao. *Map 2, C11, p249* Approaching its 100th year, this old-fashioned perfume shop is still going strong.

**El Rastrillo**, C Iparraguirre 42, Bilbao. *Map 2, G8, p249* Characterful second-hand barn selling everything including several kitchen sinks.

**Gorostiaga**, C Victor s/n, Bilbao. *Map 1, D2, p247* A serious hat shop, with all a Basque could ask for, including berets.

**Hobby's**, Gran Vía 57, Bilbao. *Map 2, F6, p248* Recreate the siege of Bilbao in Airfix or build a Basque fishing trawler from little pieces. The toy soldiers include figures of Hitler and Mussolini.

**La Condonuría**, Artekale 11, Bilbao. *Map 1, E4, p247* Novelty condoms and other Catholic fun.

**Segunda Mano**, C Prudencio María Verástegui 14, Vitoria, **T** 945-270007. An amazing barn-sized second-hand shop with everything from books to grand pianos and skis to confessionals.

Sport is big in the Basque lands. Football is an obsession, and strongly connected to the political situation: a win for Athletic Bilbao over Real Madrid, the darlings of the Spanish establishment, carries meaning far beyond the pitch. Similarly, great importance is placed on traditional Basque sports. These tend to be fairly unreconstructed tests of strength, such as wood-chopping, or the alarming stone-lifting, in which stocky *harrijasotzaileak* dead-lift weights which can exceed 300 kg; you can almost feel the hernias popping out. The best places to see these sports are at village fiestas (see Festivals, p195). The best known Basque sport, is *pelota*, or *jai alai*, played on a three-sided court. In the most common version, two teams of two hit the ball with their hands against the walls seeking to prevent the other team from returning it. The ball is far from soft; after a long career players' hands resemble winning entries in a root-vegetable show. Variations of the game are *pelota a pala*, using bats, and *cesta punta*, using a wickerwork glove that can propel the ball at frightening speeds.

Bullfighting is big during the summer *fiestas*. Bilbao is the best place to see a *corrida* but tickets are tricky to get. Many of the small towns have other bovine events during their *fiestas*, one involves teams of two attempting to put brass rings on a cow's horns.

With its long coast and green hills, Euskadi is made for outdoor activities. Cycling, horse trekking, watersports, and walking are well-catered for and rewarding. Cycling in particular is popular; when the professional circuit comes to the area, the country roads become full of enthused *cuadrillas* of friends, racing each other through the rural landscape. Miguel Indurain, possibly the greatest road cyclist of all time, is a legend (he was born in Navarra). His achievement of five consecutive Tours de France is unmatched.

▶▶ *See Tours, p27, for companies organizing excursions, and Bilbao, p49, for football and bullfights.*

## Cycling

**Federación Vasca de Ciclismo**, Paseo Anoeta 12, San Sebastián, **T** 943-457069.   The controlling body for cycling in Euskadi is very helpful for all things two-wheeled.

## Horse racing

**Hipódromo**, C Camino, San Sebastián, **T** 943-423698. South east of town.    The short but high-quality racing season runs in April and May.

## Pelota

**Federación Vasca de Pelota**, **T** 94-6818108.  The controlling body for all pelota in Euskadi. The website lists upcoming events in slightly shambolic fashion. Most courts have matches on Saturday and Sunday evenings. Confusingly, the seasons vary from town to town, but there's always something on somewhere.

## Athletic Bilbao

So this Bilbaíno is in a bar chatting with a friend and asks him:

-Did you hear that they've spent 100 million on El Guggenheim? The friend thinks for a while:

-Well, as long as he bangs in a few goals that's not too bad…

Rarely is a football team loved as deeply as Athletic Club. A Basque symbol in the same league as the Gernika oak, the team, as a matter of principle, only fields Basque players. Astonishingly, they have remained very competitive in arguably the strongest league in the world and have never been relegated. They have won 24 Spanish Cups, and the championship eight times, more than any other club bar the two Madrid giants and Barcelona.

Athletic Club grew out of the cultural exchange that was taking place in the late 19th century between Bilbao and the UK. British workers brought football to Bilbao, and Basques went to Britain to study engineering. In the early years, Athletic fielded many British players, and their strip was modelled on Sunderland's, where many of the miners were from. Games are usually on Sundays at 1700 (see San Mamés, p49.

## Trekking

There are numerous riding schools in the Basque region. Alava is the best province for trekking. Tourist offices will provide details, or try:

**Artziniega Rutas a Caballo**, **T** 945-396060. Alavan organization specializing in trekking expeditions.

**Club Hípico Okendo**, **T** 945-898098.  Another Alavan riding club organizing excursions.

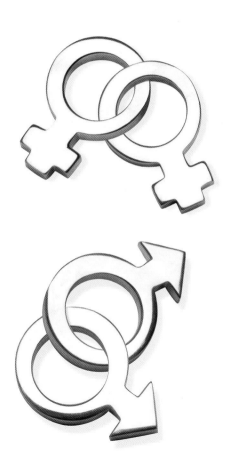

Euskadi's political awareness and antipathy to Spanish conservatism means that the cities at least are among the most tolerant in the peninsula. While there's not a scene to compare with the bigger cities of Barcelona or Madrid, there are plenty of gay and lesbian venues, and several organizations. Overt displays of homophobia are rare, and couples on the street shouldn't encounter any unpleasantness, at least in the cities. Gay tourism has increased dramatically in Bilbao since the opening of the Guggenheim, and it has the busiest and best scene. San Sebastián, particularly in summer, also sees plenty of activity. Vitoria is quieter but still has a handful of places to go. The 'pink zone' in Bilbao is across the river from the Casco Viejo near the Puente de la Merced. The Casco Viejo has a few options, which are less scene-y.

## Bars and clubs

**Badulake**, C Hernani 10. Bilbao. *Map 1, G1, p247* Weekend cabaret shows and other regular events.

**Bar Rio**, C Eduardo Dato 20, Vitoria, **T** 945-230067. A decent café with outdoor tables by day, and one of the last bars to shut at night, when it caters to a good-natured gay/straight crowd. Original live music on Thursday nights.

**Café Bizitza**, C Torre 1. Bilbao. *Metro: Casco Viejo. Map 1, E2, p247* Chilled predominantly gay bar with a Basque political slant.

**Café Lamiak**, C Pelota 8. Bilbao. *Map 1, F2, p247* A relaxed two-floor forum, the sort of place a literary genre, pressure group, or world-famous funk band might start out. Mixed crowd.

**Cairo Stereo Club**, C Aldabe 9, Vitoria. Excellent Vitorian club with excellent and innovative DJs and a mixed crowd. During the week they often show cult movies or hold theme parties. Mixed.

**Congreso**, Muelle de Uribitarte 4. Bilbao. *Open Fri and Sat nights Map 2, B9, p249* A classic *bakalao* and house venue, hardly cutting edge but a mainstay of the Bilbao scene. Doesn't really get into its stride until 0400 or so. Mixed crowd.

**Conjunto Vacío**, C Muelle de la Merced 4. *Map 2, F2, p248* Empty by name and packed by nature, at least from about 0200 on Friday and Saturday nights. The music is light *bakalao*, the crowd mixed and good-looking, drinks horrendously expensive, but entry free.

**Distrito 9**, Alameda Rekalde 18. Bilbao *Map 2, D7, p249* Still probably the best spot in Bilbao for house music. Goes very late and is quite a dressy scene. Drag shows and a €10 cover.

**Holl-Berri**, C Amistad 6, Bilbao.  *Metro: Abando.  Map 2, C11, p249*   Near the station, a popular spot for drinks, dancing and cruising.

**Ku, Monte Igueldo s/n**. San Sebastián.   Atop the Igueldo hill is one of the city's more glamorous discos, with a smart mixed crowd. Usually goes later than anywhere.

**Mykonos**, C General Castillo 4, Bilbao.  *Map 1, G1, p247*   Another pink zone option with back room and video lounge.

**Swing**, C Bastiturri 1, Vitoria, T 945-281372. A reasonable lesbian club playing comfortable pop and techno to a mixed crowd.

**Tapioca**, C Sancho El Sabio 22, Vitoria, **T** 945-247471.   A relaxed and fairly funky club with music from soul through to soft house. Open until 0500 at weekends. Interesting decoration includes exhibitions by young local artists. Mixed.

## Organizations

The principal gay and lesbian organisation in Euskadi is EHGAM, whose main office is in Bilbao.

**Aldarte**, C Barroeta Aldamar 7, Bilbao, **T** 944-237296.  *Map 2, B11, p249*   Resource centre for the gay and lesbian community in Bilbao, with information, social events, and support.

**EHGAM**, Escalinatas de Solokoetxe 4, Bilbao, **T** 944-150719.  *Map 2, D4, p249*   A good set-up whose happy folk help with any information on gay and lesbian culture and life in Euskadi.

Kids are kings in Spain, and Euskadi is no exception. They are a highly recommended travel accessory to ensure friendly service, get tables in full restaurants, meet local people, and much more. There's never a problem taking children anywhere; the locals do, and it's usual for children to accompany parents on a Friday night out; you'll often see them playing in and out of bars at two in the morning. The most enjoyable place in Euskadi for children is San Sebastián. The relaxed atmosphere, long beachfront, with a beautiful traditional merry-go-round, and pedestrian old town all make for a hassle-free holiday. Bilbao has less to offer younger children, but the seaside isn't far, and the castle of Butrón will intrigue. It's worth staying in the Casco Viejo; the traffic-free zone (except in the mornings) means more freedom.

# Bilbao/Bilbo

**Artxanda**, p39   Family atmosphere, and a fun funicular ride.

**Athletic Bilbao**,  p49   The Bilbao football team plays to a colourful crowd. The atmosphere is fabulous and very family-oriented, although kids under 10 might be a bit intimidated.

**Casco Viejo**, p33   The evening streetlife is fascinating, with plenty of buskers, living statues, and a family atmosphere.

*San Sebastián's promenade has lost none of its belle époque feel, when kings and queens strolled up and down the beachfront. Children enjoy the beautifully old-fashioned carousel.*

**Castillo del Butrón**, p58  This fairytale-style castle just outside Bilbao has all the bits a proper castle should have, and is stocked with dummies to bring things to life.

**Lekeitio**, p72  This friendly coastal town has all the action, sights, and smells of a real fishing town, as well as beaches.

**Puente de Vizcaya**, p56  The transporter bridge is very cool and the walkway 50 m above gives great views over the estuary, and is safe for all pre-vertigo ages.

## San Sebastián/Donostia

**Aquarium**, p86  The walk-through tank is fascinating, sharks get fed twice daily, and the ghostly stingrays are equally watchable.

**Miramon Kutxaespacio**, p94  The hands-on science museum has plenty of things to push and pull, and computer activities. The attached planetarium is a good show – phone ahead to beat the queues.

**Monte Igueldo**, p84  A traditional funfair with great views and a funicular ride up the hill. A few rides and a haunted house.

Kids

## Airline information

**Iberia**, C Ercilla 20, Bilbao, T 944-245506; C Bengoetxea 3, San Sebastián, T 943423586; Av Gasteiz 84, Vitoria, T 945-224142; **Spanair**, Aeropuerto de Bilbao, T 944-869498;   **British Airways**, Aeropueto de Bilbao, T 944-710523; **Airport contact numbers**: Bilbao  T 90-5505505;  San Sebastián T 943-668500;  Vitoria T 945-163591.

## Banks and ATMs

All ATMs accept most global cards. There's a branch of **BBK** at Bilbao airport. Banking hours: Monday-Friday 0830-1400, often open in the afternoon and Saturday mornings, except in summer.

## Bicycle hire

Surprisingly, facilities for the hire of bicycles are few and far between. In smaller towns the local cycle shop will usually let you use one for a reasonable fee. The **youth hostel**, p129, and the **Hotel Nervión**, p126, both hire bikes, but normally only to guests, although they might be persuaded. In Getxo, **Tsunami**, at the marina, T 944-606503, rent bicycles but charge an outrageous €31 for a day. **Bici Rent Donosti**, Av de la Zurriola 22, San Sebastián, T 943-279260, 652775526. 0900 till 2100 every day, this shop on Gros beach rents bikes by the hour and by the day (€18). **Ludoland**, C Herrería 25, Vitoria, T 945-122198, €10 per day, but, the bikes are often all gone.

## Car hire

**Atesa**, C Sabino Arana 9, Bilbao, T 944-423290; Aeropuerto de Bilbao, T 944-533340; Portal de Betoño 11, Vitoria, T 945-271012, www.atesa.es   Cheaper but less efficient than the multis. **Avis**, Av Doctor Areilza 34, Bilbao, T 944-275760, Aeropuerto de Bilbao, T 944-869648; C Triunfo 2, San Sebastián, T 943-461556;  Av Gasteiz, Vitoria, T 945-247783; www.avis.com  **Europcar**, Av Licenciado Poza 56, T 944-422226; Aeropuerto de Bilbao,

T944710133; Estación del Norte, San Sebastián, T 943-322304;
C Adriano VI 29, Vitoria, T 945-200433, www.europcar.com
**Hertz**, C Doctor Achucarro 10, Bilbao, T 944-153677; Aeropuerto
de Bilbao, T 944-530931; C Zubieta 5, San Sebastián, T 943-461084;
Pasaje de las Antillas 12, Vitoria, T945200168, www.hertz.com

## Consulates
**Britain**: T-94 4157600; **Eire**: T 944-912575; **France**: T 944-249000;
**Germany**: T 944-238585; **Portugal**: T 944-354540; **South Africa**:
T 944-641124. **US representative**: Madrid embassy,
T 91-5872200.

## Credit card lines
**Amex**: T902375637; **Mastercard**: T900971231; **Visa**: T900951125.

## Dentists
Henao 7, 48009, Bilbao, T 94 424 2980; Portal Gamarra, 1 Edif Deva.
3º pta, Ofic 306  01013 Vitoria, T 94 526 2855.

## Disabled
**Bidaideak**, T 944-234474, www.bidaideak.org, is an organization
for the disabled based in Bilbao

## Doctors
Clínica San Sebastián, c Rafael Ibarra 25, Bilbao, T 944-755000;
Santiago, 7-1º, 01002 Vitoria, T 94 525 8233; Paseo Francia,
1220012 San Sebastian, T 94 327 6300.

## Electricity
Spain runs on 220V, as does most of Europe, with a two-pin plug.

## Emergency numbers
The emergency number is 112. Dialling 091 will patch you through
to the local police force, while 085 will get an ambulance.

## Hospitals
**Hospital de Basurto**, Av Montevideo 18, Bilbao, T 944-006000, Metro: San Mamés; **Hospital Nuestra Señora de Arantzazu**, Av Doctor Begiristain 115, San Sebastián, T 943-007000; **Hospital Txagorritxu**, C José Atxotegui s/n, Vitoria, T 945-007000.

## Internet
**Laser Internet**, C Sendeja 5, Bilbao, T 944-453509. Monday-Friday 1030-0230; Saturday/Sunday 1100-0230, €0.05 per minute. Photocopier and fax services also. **El Señor de la Red**, Alameda de Rekalde 14, T 944-237425. €2 per hour. **Web Press**, C Barrancua 11, Monday-Sunday 1000-2230. **Donosti-Net**, C Embeltrán 2, San Sebastián, C San Jerónimo 8, T 943-429497. An internet café in the heart of the old town which also offers a left-luggage service. 0900-2300 daily. €3.30 per hour. **Link Internet**, C San Antonio 31, Vitoria, T 945-130484, €2.10 per hour, Monday-Friday 1000-1400, 1730-2130; Saturday 1030-1400.

## Language schools
**Instituto Hemingway**, C Bailén 5, Bilbao, T 944-167901, www.institutohemingway.com **Lacunza Escuela Internacional**, Camino de Mundaiz 8, San Sebastián, T 943-326680, www.lacunza.com

## Laundry
**Tintoreria Lavaclin**, Campo de Volantín 15, Bilbao, bag wash for €10. **Wash'n Dry**, C Iparragirre 6, San Sebastián, T 943-293150.

## Left luggage
There are consignas at all the major train stations in the region.

## Libraries
**Biblioteca Municipal**, C Bidebarrieta 4, Bilbao, T 944-156930. Monday-Friday 0930-2100, Saturday 0930-1400.

## Lost property

There's a lost property line, T 944-204981, but it's worth contacting the local police station too.

## Media

The press is generally of a high journalistic standard. The national dailies **El Pais**, **El Mundo**, and the rightist **ABC** lose out in the Basque lands to **El Correo**, a quality Bilbao-based syndicated chain. **El Diario Vasco** is another Basque daily, while **Egin** and **Deia** are papers half published in Euskara with a blatantly nationalistic bias.

## Pharmacies (late night)

Pharmacies in Euskadi are on a rotating late-opening shift.

## Police

Emergencies: 112;  Local police: 091.  Police stations: **Policia Municipal Bilbao**, C Luis Briñas 14, T 944-205000. **Policia Municipal San Sebastián**, C Larramendi 10, T 943-450000. **Policía Municipal Vitoria**, C Aguirrelanda s/n, T 945-161111

## Post offices

Main post offices open Monday-Friday 0830-2030, some Saturday 0930-1400. Stamps can be bought at post offices or tobacconists (*estancos*). **Bilbao main post office**: Alameda Urquijo 19. **San Sebastián**: Paseo de Francia s/n. **Vitoria**: Calle de Postas 9.

## Public holidays

See Festivals, p195,  for local holidays. Euskadi-wide holidays are: 1st January: New Year; 19 March: San José; Maundy Thursday, Good Friday, Easter Monday; 1 May: Labour Day; 25 July: Santiago; 31 July: San Ignacio (not Alava); 5 August: Virgen Blanca (Alava only); 15 August: Asunción; 12 October: National Day; 1 November: All Saints' Day; 6 December: Constitution Day; 25 December: Christmas Day.

## Religious services

There's an Anglican church in the British cemetery not far from Bilbao airport, T 944-781029/605722281 for service times.

## Telephone

The international dialling code for Spain is +34. To make an international call from Spain, dial 00 followed by the country code. Calls within Spain begin with a three digit area code, dialled in all cases. Mobile numbers begin with 6. Public phones accept coins and cards, and all have international direct dialling. *Locutorios* (call centres) are few and far between.

## Time

Spain is one hour ahead of GMT, and puts its clocks forward and back at the same time as Britain and the rest of Europe.

## Toilets

Public toilets are reasonably common, some coin operated. Bar staff will rarely have a problem with you using theirs, if you ask. Toilets are indicated by: *Aseos, Baños, Komunak, Servicios,* or *HHSS*.

## Transport enquiries

**Bilbao bus station**: T 944-395077; **RENFE** station: T 90-2240202; **Euskotren**: T 90-2543210; **FEVE**: T 944-232266.
**San Sebastián buses**: **ALSA**: T 943-462360; **PESA**: T 90-2101210; **Continental**: T 943-469074; **RENFE** station: T 943-426430; **Euskotren**: T 943-013500. **Vitoria bus station**: T 945-258400; **RENFE** station: T 90-2240202.

## Travel agents

**Eroski Bidaiak**, C Licenciado Poza 10, Bilbao, T 944-439012 ; C Igentea 2, San Sebastián, T 943-429740. **Viajes Ecuador**, Gran Vía 81, Bilbao, T 90-2207070; Av Gasteiz 34, Vitoria, T 945-132144.

# A sprint through history

**Prehistory**     Evidence of habitation in the Basque region goes back more than 50,000 years. Cave paintings suggest a continuous habitation since 10,000 BC

**71 BC**     The Roman general Pompey campaigns in the area against the rogue general Quintus Sertorius, who had set himself up as a local warlord. He founded Pamplona, naming it after himself.

**581 AD**     The Visigoths fight several battles against the Basques, trying to pacify the peninsula.

**778**     Charlemagne campaigns in Navarra and, returning to France, his rear guard is ambushed by Basques in the Pyrenees. The resulting battle gave rise to the *Chanson de Roland*.

**1004**     Sancho the Great ascends the throne of Navarra, founds Vitoria and unites a large region.

**1200**     Alava and much of Guipúzcoa are taken by the crown of Castile, where they remain.

**1300**     Bilbao granted its town charter by Don Diego López de Haro. It begins to flourish as a port for exporting goods produced in the interior.

**1522**     Juan Sebastián Elkano, from Getaria, becomes the first to circumnavigate the globe after the death of his captain Magellan in the Philippines.

**1534**     The Basque dandy Iñigo de Loyola, recovering from horrible injuries, has a series of religious revelations and founds the Company of Jesus, or Jesuits.

**1728**     The Real Compañia Guipúzcoana de Caracas is founded to monopolize the import of chocolate .

| 1813 | The Peninsular War; the French garrison in San Sebastián was finally defeated. British and Portuguese troops set fire to the town, most of which was destroyed. The French are later routed just outside Vitoria, signalling an end to their Spanish campaign. |
| 1833-39 | Arising over a dispute over succession, the first Carlist war was a civil war heavily involving the Basques. The conservative Carlists, whose stronghold was the Basque agricultural towns, besieged liberal Bilbao, eventually unsuccessfully. |
| 1841 | As punishment for their support of the Carlists, the liberal government under the victorious queen more or less end Basque autonomy after the war. |
| 1845 | The beginning of Bilbao's big boom; Vizcaya becomes the premier source of haematite, the most effective ore for the steelmaking processes. |
| 1872 | Second Carlist war |
| 1876 | End of second Carlist war – the Basque *fueros* (privileges) are completely abolished. |
| 1890 | Sabino Arana publishes a work that becomes the foundation of Basque nationalism, and devises the *ikurriña* (the Basque flag) and the name Euskadi. |
| 1903 | The Great Strike of Bilbao, the good times end. |
| 1920 | Massive decline in iron output, which halved between 1913-29. |

| | |
|---|---|
| 1936 | The Spanish Civil War; the first Basque government is installed under the leadership of Aguirre on October 7 after he pledges to support the Republicans. |
| 1937 | The brutal bombings of civilians at Durango and Gernika are carried out by Nationalist forces in late April. In June, Bilbao is taken by the Nationalists and the Basques surrender, many fight on in other regions, and against Hitler in World War Two. |
| 1952 | ETA founded by young Basques disenchanted with European and American recognition of Franco. |
| 1973 | Admiral Carrero Blanco, prime minister and Franco's right hand killed by an ETA car bomb; an assassination that met with massive public support. |
| 1975 | Franco dies after nearly four decades of repression of the Basque region, in retribution for their Republicanism during the Civil War. |
| 1980 | Semi-autonomy is granted to the Basque region, and separately to Navarra. The regions have power to raise their own taxes, have their own police force, and control public works and education. Many Basques are satisfied with this concession, but ETA continue their programme of violence. |
| 1997 | The Guggenheim museum opens in Bilbao. |
| 2002 | Batasuna, the political party widely seen as a backer of ETA activities are banned after a custom-designed bill passed by the Spanish parliament. |

# Art and architecture

**Romanesque (11th-12th century)**

A fusion of styles combining features of Roman, Visigothic, and local architecture, mainly spread through the church. Vaulted stone roofs made for less flammable buildings, which usually have small round-arched door and window openings, often featuring carved decoration. Even the larger structures have a warm and homely aspect, contrasting with the more austere and remote Gothic style that followed. There are numerous small Romanesque chapels in the Basque countryside, one of the grander examples is the basilica of San Prudencio in Vitoria (Armentia).

**Gothic (13th to mid-16th centuries)**

Inspired by France and boosted by the unification of the peninsula, its primary features are pointed arches and rib-vaulting, which had been used sparingly in Romanesque buildings. Advances in engineering allowed lighter, higher structures, supported by exterior 'flying' buttresses. Becoming ever lighter and more elaborate it incorporated stained glass and intricate carved sculptures. Gothic art, characterized by ornate coloured *retablos* (altarpieces), developed primarily through the religious medium. While today Gothic architecture is widely considered supreme in elegance and execution, the term was originally pejorative, meaning 'barbarous'.

| | |
|---|---|
| **Renaissance (16th century)** | The Spanish Renaissance was influenced by Italian artists and became more grandiose, intricate and, some would say, pompous over time. Vitoria and Oñati has some excellent examples. |
| **Baroque (17th-18th century)** | The period was a time of great architectural and artistic genius in Spain and the Basque country. The Churrigueresque architectural style went even further down the ornamental path. Baroque *retablos* were frequently gilded and seem in extreme contrast to the Gothic churches they're often in. |
| **Neoclassicism (mid 18th-19th centuries)** | A reaction against the excesses of Baroque, this sober style called on classical models to produce severe but harmonious civil and religious architecture, such as the Plaza Nueva in Bilbao. Much of the 'new towns' of the Basque cities are in this style. |
| **Art Nouveau and Art Deco (late 19th century)** | Art Nouveau aimed to bring art back to life and back to the everyday. Using naturalistic motifs to create whimsical façades and *objets*, the best Art Nouveau works combined elegance with fancy. Art Deco developed between the World Wars and was based on geometric forms, using new materials and colour combinations to create a popular style. San Sebastián is a temple to Art Nouveau, and, like Bilbao, has many good examples of Deco. |
| **Modern** | Inhibited or in exile during Franco's turgid time at the crease, Basque art and architecture has flourished since his demise. The Basque sculptors Chillida and Oteiza are globally admired, while the Guggenheim Museum, Artium and Kursaal have set the architectural tone for the 21st century. |

# Books

A watershed in Basque writing came in the late 19th century with the fiery works of Sabino Arana. Littered with inaccuracies and untruths, much of his writing reads more like propaganda than literature, but it created modern Basque nationalism; since then it has been difficult for Basque writings to avoid the issue.

The gentle fables of Samaniego are probably the best known Basque literary works prior to that time. Unamuno's massive corpus of writing ranged from philosophy to poetry, novels and journalism. Written as a young man living in Bilbao, the work reflects the atmosphere of the time, when earnest discussions in cafés fuelled the world of the arts. This has made something of a comeback in recent years. Franco's rigidity and banning of Euskera hit this scene hard. Pío Baroja is one of the few authors to stand out from the mid 20th century; his image-filled novels often deeply reflect Basque rural life. Blas de Otero, who had a complex love for Bilbao, spent most of his writing life overseas. The Basque government is aware of the importance of the arts, and encourages writers with cultural grants. An ongoing problem is *politiization*; it is next to impossible for a new writer to avoid rigorous dissection of his works and being labelled as pro or anti Basque nationalism.

**Atxaga**, **B**, *Obabakoak* (1994), Vintage Books. A dreamlike series of anecdotes making up a novel by a well-respected contemporary Basque author. Drawn from Basque heritage rather than about Basque culture. Individual and profound.

**Baroja**, **P**, *The Tree of Knowledge* (1911). While mostly set in Madrid and Valencia, this is the best introduction to this powerful Basque novelist.

**Barrenechea**, **T**, *The Basque Table* (1998), Harvard Common Press. A cookbook with tons of traditional Basque recipes.

**Carr**, **R** (ed), *Spain: A History (2000)*, Oxford University Press. An interesting compilation of recent writing on Spanish history, with plenty of perspective on Basque issues.

**Kurlansky**, **M**, *The Basque History of the World (1999)*, Vintage Press. A likeable introduction to what makes the Basques tick, what they eat, what they've done, and what they're like. Informal and fireside style.

**Nooteboom**, **C**, *Roads to Santiago (1992)*, The Harvill Press. Although this offbeat travelogue doesn't have massive amounts on the Basque country, it is one of the best travel books around, soulful, literary, and entertaining.

**Steer**, **G**, *The Tree of Guernica (1938)*, Hodder and Stoughton. Written by a reporter who was an eyewitness to the atrocity of the bombing, this is of most interest for an evocative description of the event itself. Steer was heavily pro-Republican.

**Thomas**, **H**, *The Spanish Civil War (1961/77)*, Penguin. The first unbiased account of the war read by many Spaniards in the censored Franco years, this is large but always readable.

**Unamuno**, **M**, *Tragic Sense of Life (1913)*, Dover Publications (1990). The anguished and heroically honest attempt by the great Basque and Salamantine philosopher to come to terms with faith and death.

**Zulaika**, **J**, *Basque Violence: Metaphor and Sacrament (2000)*, University of Nevada Press. An academic but intriguing exploration of the roots of Basque nationalist feeling, and the progression to violence.

## The Philosopher's Last Stand

One of Bilbao's most famous sons was Miguel de Unamuno, poet, philosopher, and academic, born in 1864 on Calle Ronda. One of the 'Generation of '98', a new wave of artists and thinkers emerging in the wake of the Spanish-American war of 1898, Unamuno was a humanist and a catholic with an idealistic love of truth; making him enemies in a Spain where political beliefs tended to come first. Many Basques still have mixed feelings about 'Don Miguel', who, although proud of being Basque, wasn't pro-independence.

In Salamanca when the Civil War broke out, Unamuno, previously a deputy in the Republic, had supported the rising, but grew more and more alarmed with the nature of the Nationalist movement.

On October 12, 1936 he presided over the Columbus day ceremony at the university, which rapidly degenerated into fascist propaganda. A professor denounced Basque and Catalan nationalism as cancers that fascism would cut out. General Millán Astray, a war veteran with one eye, one arm, and missing fingers on the other one, continued with more empty rhetoric to a hall resounding to the popular Falangist slogan "long live death". Unamuno rose to close the meeting. "At times to be silent is to lie", he said. "I want to comment on the speech – to give it that name – of the professor. Let's ignore the personal affront implied. I am a Basque from Bilbao. The bishop (pro-fascist) next to me is Catalan, from Barcelona". He then moved on to Astray, whom he harshly criticized, and who responded by crying "Death to intellectuals". Guns were pointed at the 72 year old, who went on: "You will win, because you have the brute force. But you will not convince. For to convince, you would need what you lack: reason and right in the struggle". Under house arrest, he died a couple of months later, it was said, of a broken heart.

# Language

## Euskara

Spanish is the main language of the Basque lands, spoken by everyone. After decades of hiding under Franco, the Basque language Euskara has come back with a bang: an evergrowing number of people are learning and using it. You'll see it everywhere; on road signs, in bars, on posters. Some of the regional towns use only Basque for naming streets, etc. It's an ancient and difficult language with no known relatives. Like Finnish, it is agglutinative, meaning roughly that distinct bits are joined on to words for each element of meaning. Whereas in Spanish, the –é at the end of *hablé,* (I spoke) denotes the tense (past), the person (first), the number (singular), mood, mode, and aspect, in Basque these are all represented by distinct additions, which results in numerous variations of a single word. People struggle with the seven cases in Latin, but Basque has a massive 20.

Euskara is pronounced as it is written, with these main exceptions: *x* is "sh", *s* is almost lisped as is the slightly harder *z* sound, *h* is usually silent. The *eu* diphthong is pronounced as a quick "ay-oo".

*¡Kaixo!* Hello
*Bai* Yes
*Ez* No
*Ongi-etorri* Welcome
*Eskerrik asko* Thank you
*Komunak* Toilets
*Hondartza* Beach
*Mesedez* Please
*Agur* Hello/goodbye
*Ardo* Wine
*Baserri* Farmhouse
*Etxe* House. Many words and names derive from this word

*Sagardotegi*  Ciderhouse
*Jatetxea*  Restaurant
*Kale*  Street
*Ostatua*  Hostal or pensión
*Parkatu*  Excuse me
*Ura*  Water
*Garagardo*  Beer

## Castellano

### Greetings, courtesies
Good morning    *buenos días*
How are you?  *¿cómo está?/¿cómo estás?*
Pleased to meet you  *mucho gusto/encantado/encantada*
What is your name?  *¿Cómo se llama?*
I am called  *me llamo…*
Excuse me/I beg your pardon/sorry  *permiso/disculpe*
I do not understand  *no entiendo*
please speak slowly  *hable despacio por favor*
I don't speak Spanish  *no hablo castellano*
Do you speak English?  *¿Habla usted inglés?*

### Money
bill  *la cuenta*
cheap  *barato*
credit card  *la tarjeta de crédito*
exchange house  *la casa de cambio, CADECA*
exchange rate  *la tasa de cambio*
expensive  *caro*
How much does it cost?  *¿Cuánto cuesta?*

### Getting around
Where is?  *¿Dónde está?*
corner  *la esquina*

How do I get to_? ¿Cómo llegar a_?
on the left/right  *a la izquierda/derecha*
straight on  *derecho*
ticket office  *la taquilla*
walk  *caminar*
When does the plane leave/arrive? ¿A qué hora sale/llega el autobus?
Where can I buy tickets?  *¿Dónde se puede comprar billetes?*

---

## Accommodation

clean/dirty towels  *las toallas limpias/sucias*
Have you got a room for two people? ¿Tiene habitación para dos personas?
Is service included? ¿Está incluido el servicio?
pillows  *las almohadas*
sheets  *las sábanas*
shower  *la ducha*
single/double  *individual/doble*
to make up/clean  *limpiar*
toilet paper  *el papel higiénico*
with private bathroom  *con baño*
with two beds  *con dos camas*

---

## Time

At half past two/ two thirty  *a las dos y media*
At a quarter to three  *a las tres menos quince*
It's seven o'clock  *son las siete*
It's twenty past six/six twenty  *son las seis y veinte*
It's five to nine  *son las nueve menos cinco*
In ten minutes  *en diez minutos*
five hours  *cinco horas*
Does it take long? ¿Tarda mucho?
We will be back at  *Regresamos a las…*
What time is it? ¿Qué hora es?

Monday *lunes*
Tuesday *martes*
Wednesday *miércoles*
Thursday *jueves*
Friday *viernes*
Saturday *sábado*
Sunday *domingo*

### Food

It is impossible to be definitive about terms used. Different regions have numerous variants

*Aceitunas* Olives
*Ajo* Garlic
*Alcachofa* Artichoke
*Alioli* A tasty sauce made from raw garlic blended with oil and egg yolk
*Almejas* Name applied to various species of small clams
*Alubias* Beans
*Anchoa* Preserved anchovy
*Angulas* Baby eels, a scarce and expensive delicacy
*Arroz* Rice
*Asado* Roast
*Bacalao* Salted cod, an emblematic Basque food. Try *al pil-pil* (Bilbao's trademark dish; a light yellow sauce made from oil garlic, and the natural gelatin of the cod). *Al ajo arriero* is mashed with garlic, parsley, and paprika.
*Berenjena* Aubergine/eggplant
*Bistek* Steak. *Poco hecho* is rare, *al punto* is medium rare, *regular* is medium, *muy hecho* is well-done to cremated
*Bonito* Atlantic bonito, a small tasty tuna fish
*Boquerones* Fresh anchovies
*Cabracho* Scorpionfish
*Cabrales* A delicious Asturian cheese similar to Roquefort

*Cacahuetes* Peanuts

*Café* Coffee. *Solo* is black, served espresso-style. *Cortado* adds a dash of milk, *con leche* more. *Americano* is a long black.

*Caña* A draught beer

*Cazuela* A stew, often of fish or seafood

*Cerdo* Pork

*Cerveza* Beer. If you want draught beer, ask for a *caña*

*Chuleta* ChuletillaChop

*Cochinillo/Lechón/Tostón* Sucking pig

*Cocido* A heavy stew, usually of meat and beans

*Cordero* Lamb

*Costillas* Ribs

*Cuajada Junket* A thin natural yoghurt eaten with honey

*Cuenta (la)* The bill

*Dorada* A species of bream (gilthead)

*Embutido* Any salami-type sausage

*Foie* Fattened liver. Often made into a thick gravy-like sauce

*Gambas* Prawns

*Garbanzo* Chickpea

*Guisado* Stewed, or a stew

*Higado* Liver

*Idiazabal* Basque sheepmilk cheese

*Kokotxas* Pieces of hake cheek and throat, cooked in a rich sauce

*Lechazo* Milk-fed lamb

*Lenguado* Sole

*Lose* Service included (it never is)

*Lubina* Sea bass

*Marisco* Shellfish

*Mejillones* Mussels

*Membrillo* Quince jelly, usually eaten with cheese

*Menestra* A vegetable stew, often seeded with ham and pork

*Menú* A set meal, usually consisting of three or more courses, bread and wine or water

*Merluza* Hake is to Spain as rice is to southeast Asia

*Morcilla*  Blood sausage

*Mosto*  Grape juice, a common option in bars

*Nécora*  Small sea crab, sometimes called a velvet crab

*Orujo*  A fiery grape spirit, added to coffee if the waiter likes you

*Pato*  Duck

*Patxarán*  Sloe-berry, but usually the liqueur made from it

*Pollo*  Chicken

*Postre*  Dessert

*Puerros*  Leeks

*Pulga*  Tiny submarine-shaped rolls that feature atop bars

*Pulpo*  Octopus

*Queso*  Cheese

*Rabo de buey*  Oxtail

*Rape*  Monkfish

*Relleno/a*  Stuffed

*Revuelto*  Scrambled eggs, usually with mushrooms or seafood

*Rodaballo*  Turbot. Pricey and toothsome

*Romana (à la)*  Fried in batter

*Sagardotegi*  Cider house

*Sal*  Salt

*Setas*  Wild mushrooms, often superb

*Sidra*  Cider

*Solomillo*  Beef fillet steak cut from the sirloin bone

*Sopa*  Soup

*Ternera*  Veal or young beef

*Trucha*  Trout

*Ttoro*  A traditional Basque fish stew or soup

*Txaka*  A mixture of mayonnaise and chopped seafood

*Txangurro*  Spider crab, superb

*Vermut*  Vermouth. Delicious when it's the bar's own

*Vizcaína (à la)*  Usually based on onions and dried peppers

*Zurito*  A short beer, useful for tapas-hopping

# Index

Bold page number denotes main entry

# Credits

**Footprint credits**

Text editor: Caroline Lascom
Series editor: Rachel Fielding

Production: Jo Morgan, Mark Thomas
In-house cartography: Claire Benison,
Kevin Feeney, Robert Lunn,
Sarah Sorensen
Proof-reading: Jane Franklin,
Emma Bryers

Design: Mytton Williams
Maps: adapted from original cartography
by Netmaps SA, Barcelona, Spain

**Photography credits**

Front cover: Imagestate
Inside: Andy Symington
Generic images: John Matchett
Back cover: Andy Symington

**Print**

Manufactured in Italy by Rotolito
Lombarda, Italy

**Publishing information**

Footprint Bilbao
1st edition
Text and maps © Footprint Handbooks
Ltd November 2002

ISBN 1 903471 45 1
CIP DATA: a catalogue record for this
book is available from the British Library

® Footprint Handbooks and the Footprint
mark are a registered trademark of
Footprint Handbooks Ltd

Published by Footprint Handbooks
6 Riverside Court
Lower Bristol Road
Bath, BA2 3DZ, UK
T +44 (0)1225 469141
F +44 (0)1225 469461
E discover@footprintbooks.com
W www.footprintbooks.com

Distributed in the USA by
Publishers Group West

# Complete title list

## Latin America & Caribbean

Latin America & Caribbean
Argentina
Barbados (P)
Bolivia
Brazil
Caribbean Islands
Central America & Mexico
Chile
Colombia
Costa Rica
Cuba
Cusco & the Inca Trail
Dominican Republic
Ecuador & Galápagos
Handbook
Guatemala Handbook
Havana (P)
Mexico
Nicaragua
Peru
Rio de Janeiro
South American
Handbook
Venezuela

## North America

Vancouver (P)
Western Canada

## Africa

Cape Town (P)
East Africa
Libya
Marrakech &
the High Atlas
Morocco
Namibia
South Africa
Tunisia
Uganda

## Middle East

Egypt
Israel
Jordan
Syria & Lebanon

## Asia

Bali
Bangkok & the Beaches
Cambodia
Goa
India
Indian Himalaya
Indonesia
Laos
Malaysia
Myanmar (Burma)
Nepal
Pakistan
Rajasthan & Gujarat
Singapore
South India
Sri Lanka
Sumatra
Thailand
Tibet
Vietnam

## Australasia

Australia
New Zealand
Sydney (P)
West Coast Australia

## Europe

Andalucía
Barcelona
Berlin (P)
Bilbao (P)
Bologna (P)
Copenhagen (P)
Croatia
Dublin (P)
Edinburgh (P)
England
Glasgow
Ireland
London
Madrid (P)
Naples (P)
Northern Spain
Paris (P)
Reykjavik (P)
Scotland
Scotland Highlands &
Islands
Spain
Turkey

(P) denotes pocket
Handbook

# For a different view…
## choose a Footprint

Over 80 Footprint travel guides
Covering more than 145 of the world's most exciting
countries and cities in Latin America, the Caribbean, Africa, Indian
sub-continent, Australasia, North America, Southeast Asia, the
Middle East and Europe.

Discover so much more…
The finest writers. In-depth knowledge. Entertaining and accessible.
Critical restaurant and hotels reviews. Lively descriptions of all the
attractions. Get away from the crowds.

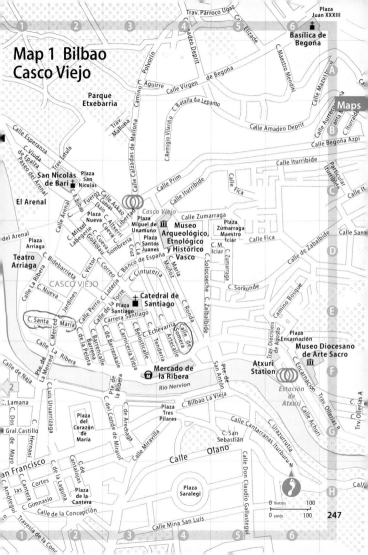

# Map 1 Bilbao
# Casco Viejo

Plaza Juan XXXIII

Basílica de Begoña

Trav. Párroco Ugaz

C. Elizalde

C. Maestro Mendiri

C. Aureolo

Maps

C. Iturribide

C. It

Parque Etxebarria

C. Aguirre    Calle Virgen    de Begoña

Camino Polvorín

C. Batalla de Lepanto

Calle Amadeo Deprit

Calle Amadeo Deprit

C. Remigio Vilariño

Calle Begoña Azpi

Trav. Mallona

C. Calzadas de Mallona

Calle Iturribide

Particular Iturribide

Calle Esperanza

C. Viuda de Epalza
Paseo del Arenal

Trav. Lotuá

Plaza San Nicolás

Calle Arenal

Calle Bilbao

Calle Askao

Calle Fueros

Cuesta de la Cueva

C. Atxeri

Calle Iturribide

C. Libertad

Calle Prim

Calle Zumárraga

Calle Fica

Calle San

San Nicolás de Bari

El Arenal

Plaza Nueva

C. Mitxel Labegerie

C. Cueva C.

C. Cueva

Itxalekri

C. Cueva Sombrería

Plaza Miguel de Unamuno

Museo Arqueológico, Etnológico y Histórico Vasco

Plaza Zumárraga Maestro Iciar

Calle Fica

Calle de Zabalbide

del Arenal

Plaza Arriaga

C. Víctor

C. Bidebarrieta

C. Correo

Cruz

Plaza Santos Juanes

C. Banco de España

C. M. Iciar

C. Zumárraga

C. Solocoeche

Teatro Arriaga

C. La Ribera

C. C. Nueva

Jardines

C. Perro

C. Loteria

C. Cinturería

C. Muñoz

C. Ronda

C. Sorkunde

Camino Bosque

CASCO VIEJO

C. Santa María

C. La Merced

Pte. de La Merced

C. Jardines

C. de la Torre

Plaza Santiago

Carrera Santiago

Catedral de Santiago

C. de Barrencalle

C. Belosticalle

C. Echevarria

C. de la Cruz

C. Comea

Calle de Artecalle

C. Zabalbide

Plaza Encarnación

Museo Diocesano de Arte Sacro

C. de Naja

C. La Merced

La Ribera

Pte. de la Ribera

C. Barrenkale

C. de la Pelota

C. Carnicería Vieja

Tendería

Pte. de San Antón

Atxuri Station

Trav. Dieciséis de Agosto

C. Encarnación

Trav. Ollerías A

Lamana

C. Dos

C. Luís Urruarrizaga

C. del Conde de Mirasol

Mercado de la Ribera

Río Nervión

C. Bilbao La Vieja

C. San Antón

Estación de Atxuri

C. Achuri

C. Ollerías A

Gral. Castillo

Hernani

Plaza del Corazón de María

C. de Arechaga

Plaza Tres Pilares

Calle Cantarranas Iturburu

C. Urazurrutia

Trv. Ollerías A

C. de Mayo

C. Anteguera

Calle Miravilla

C. San Sebastián

Calle

San Francisco

C. Cantera

Cortes

C. Gimnasio

Plaza de la Cantera

C. de Cantalojas

Calle Olano

Plaza Saralegi

Calle Don Claudio Gallástegui

Travesía de la Conc

Calle de la Concepción

Calle Mina San Luis

0 metres    100
0 yards    100

**247**

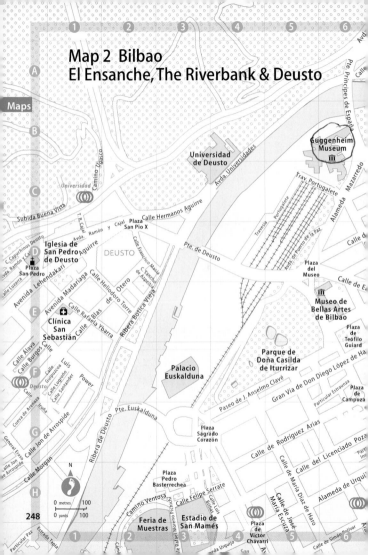

# Map 2 Bilbao
# El Ensanche, The Riverbank & Deusto

Guggenheim
Museum

Universidad
de Deusto

Avda. Universidades

Trav. Portugalete

Universidad

Camino Ugasco

Subida Buena Vista

T.R.Cajal

Avda. Ramón y Cajal Calle Hermanos Aguirre

Plaza
San Pio X

Travesía Portugalete

Alameda Mazarredo

Calle de E

C. Capuchino Deusto

Iglesia de
San Pedro
de Deusto

Avda. Ramón y Cajal

C. Sancho
de Azpeita

C. Francisco Macía

Pte. de Deusto

Avda. de Puerto de la Paz

Plaza
del
Museo

Calle de E

Plaza
San Pedro

DEUSTO

Avda. Lehendakari

Avenida Madariaga

Calle Heliodoro Otero

Ribera Botica Vieja

Museo de
Bellas Artes
de Bilbao

Calle Luzarra

Clínica
San
Sebastián

Avenida Madariaga

Calle Rafaela Ybarra

Calle Blas

Torre

Plaza
de
Teófilo
Guiard

Calle Álava

Calle Burgos

Calle

Calle Guipúzcoa

Calle Luis

Calle Santander

Calle Logroño

Power

Parque de
Doña Casilda
de Iturrizar

Plaza
de
Campuza

Deusto

Calle de Aretxaga

Cueva de
Iruña

Palacio
Euskalduna

Paseo de J. Anselmo Clavé

Gran Via de Don Diego López de Ha

Particular Extraunza

General Ec

Calle Jon de Arróspide

Ribera de Deusto

Pte. Euskalduna

Plaza
Ságrado
Corazón

Calle de Rodríguez Arias

Pan

Calle Jon
de Arróspide

Calle Morgan

N

Plaza
Pedro
Basterrechea

Calle de María Díaz de Haro

Alameda de Urqui

Calle del Licenciado Poza

0 metres    100

0 yards    100

Calle de José
María Escuza

Camino Ventosa

Calle Felipe Serrate

Calle Luis
Briñas

Calle de Simón Bol

Particular Paz    Estrada Tapia

Feria de
Muestras

Calle Rafael Moreno Pichichi

Estadio de
San Mamés

Plaza
de
Víctor Chávarri

Alameda Urquijo

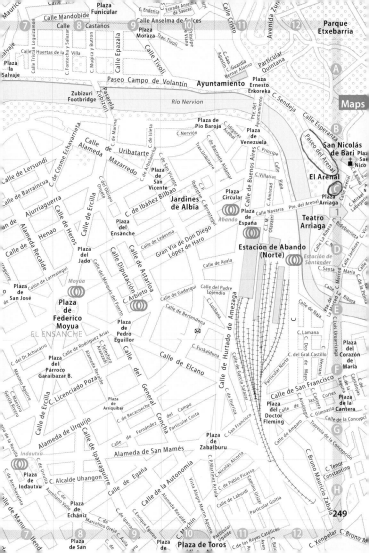

Maps

249

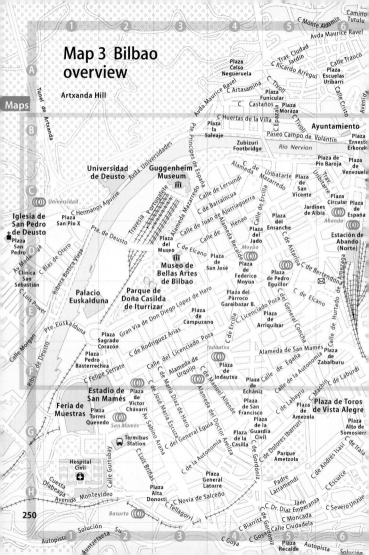

# Map 3 Bilbao overview

Artxanda Hill

Tunel de Artxanda

Universidad

Iglesia de San Pedro de Deusto

Plaza San Pedro

Av María Díaz

Clínica San Sebastián

Blas de Otero

C Luis Power

Ribera Botica Vieja

Pte. Euskalduna

Ribª de Deusto

Calle Morgan

Universidad de Deusto

Plaza San Pío X

C Hermanos Aguirre

Pte. de Deusto

Travesía Portugalete

Avda. Universidades

Pte. Príncipes de España

Plaza fa Salvaje

Plaza Celso Negueruela

Avda Maurice Ravel

C Artasamina

C Huertas de la Villa

Plaza Funicular

Castaños

C Tívoli

C Ricardo Arregui

C Tívoli

Plaza Moraza

Avda Maurice Ravel

Trav. Ciudad Jardín

Plaza Escuelas Uribarri

Calle Trauco

Calle Cristo

Avenida

Camino Tutulu

C Monte Aldamiz

Guggenheim Museum

Alameda Mazarredo

Zubizuri Footbridge

Paseo Campo de Volantín

Ayuntamiento

Río Nervión

Plaza Ernesto Erkoreka

Plaza de Pío Baroja

Plaza de Venezuela

Calle de Lersundi

C de Barraincua

Calle de Juan de Ajuriaguerra

Calle de Elcano

Plaza del Museo

C de Elcano

Henao

Alameda Recalde

Plaza de San José

Museo de Bellas Artes de Bilbao

Palacio Euskalduna

Parque de Doña Casilda de Iturrizar

Gran Vía de Don Diego López de Haro

C de Rodríguez Arias

Plaza Sagrado Corazón

Plaza Pedro Basterrechea

C Felipe Serrate

Plaza Torres Quevedo

Estadio de San Mamés

Feria de Muestras

San Mamés

Termibus Station

C Luis Briñas

Hospital Civil

Cuesta Olabeaga

Avenida Montevideo

Plaza Alta Donosti

Basurto

Plaza de Federico Moyúa

Plaza del Párroco Garaibazar B.

C de Ercilla

C Licenciado Poza

Plaza de Campuzano

Alameda de Urquijo

C de General Concha

Plaza de Arriquibar

Indautxu

Plaza de Indautxu

C del Licenciado Poza

C de María Díaz de Haro

C de José María Escuza

Av Sabino Arana

C del General Eguía

C de la Autonomía Arelza

Plaza de la Casilla

Plaza de la Guardia Civil

Plaza de San Francisco

Plaza de Echaniz

Alameda de San Mamés

Alameda del Doctor Areilza

C de Gordóniz

Plaza General Latorre

C Novia de Salcedo

C Tellagorri

Alameda de Egaña

Plaza de Zabalburu

Calle de la Autonomía

C de Labayru

Plaza de Amezola

Parque Ametzola

C de Dolores Ibarruri

Padre Larramendi

Plaza Alto de Somosierra

Plaza de Toros de Vista Alegre

Machín

C de Laburdi

C de Andrés Isasi

C de Irala

C Escurce

Jaén

C de Díaz Emperanza

C Moncada

C Biarritz

C Goya

Calle Ciudadela

C Goya

C Gordóniz

C Severo Unzue

Plaza Recalde

Autopista

Solución

Alameda Mazarredo

C de Uribatarte

Plaza de San Vicente

Plaza de Ercilla

Plaza del Ensanche

Plaza del Jado

Moyúa

Plaza de Pedro Eguillor

Plaza de Federico Moyúa

C de Astarloa

C de Bertendona

C de Elcano

Calle de Hurtado de Amézaga

Alameda de San Mamés

Plaza Circular

Jardines de Albia

Plaza de España

Estación de Abando (Norte)

Abando

Estación de Abando (Norte)

Plaza Ernesto Erkoreka

Trav. Uribitarte

**Ayuntamiento**

**250**

C Dr. Díaz Emperanza

Autopista

Aurtzetxeta

Su

250

# Map 4 San Sebastián centre

Paseo Nuevo

Paseo Nuevo

Playa de Zurriola

Avenida Zurriola

Pl. Padre Claret
Pl. Lapurdi
Plaza
Chofre
Plaza
Bernini
C. Chofre
Plaza
Yalarrosa
Pl. Segundo
C. Francisco
Plaza
Balleneros
C. Bergia
GROS
Plaza
Catalana
C. Gran
C. Iñigo
C. Calle
C. Ramón y Cajal
C. Zabaleta
Plaza Cataluña
C. Padre Larroca
Plaza Biteri
C. Luises
C. Trueba
C. Miguel Imaz
C. Peña y Goñi
Calle Leku
C. Nueva
Ronda Sta. Catalina
C. Tomás Gros
Pre. Sta. Catalina
Plaza Euskadi

Plaza
Chofre
Cno. San
Cristóbal
Calle Aldakonea
Camino Concepcion
Paseo Duque de Mandas
Plaza Teresa de Calcuta
Plaza Hirukada
Plaza Blas Otero
María Dolores Aguirre

Avenida de Francia

Paseo de Francia
Pre. María Cristina
Estación del Norte
Árbol de Guernica
Prim

Palacio de Congresos

Paseo Ramón María Lili

Paseo Ramón María Lili

Museo San Telmo
Iglesia San Vicente
Po. Manuel de Salamanca
C. Zuloaga
C. Aldamar
C. 31 de Agosto
C. Narrica
C. Esterlines
C. Mayor
C. Campanario
C. Angel
Mercado de la Bretxa
PARTE
Oficina de Turismo
Teatro Victoria Eugenia
Hotel María Cristina
Po. Rep. Argentina
Pso. de los Fueros
Jardines de Oquendo
Plaza Gipuzkoa
C. Legazpi
C. Garibay
C. Bergara
C. Idiaquez
C. Churruca
Avenida de la Libertad
C. San Marcial
C. Guetaria
C. Loyola
C. Elcano
CENTRO
Catedral del Buen Pastor
Calle Martín Pl. del Buen Pastor
C. Urbieta
C. Easo
C. San Martín
C. Arrasate
C. Reyes Católicos

C. Hernani

C. Miramar

Paseo de la Concha

Basílica de Sta. María del Coro
Castillo de la Mota
Monte Urgull
Museo Naval
Puerto
El Muelle
Ayuntamiento
Parque Alderdi Eder

Aquarium
Subida al Castillo
Paseo Nuevo
Jacques Cousteau

Bahía de la Concha

Playa de la Concha

253

# Map 5 San Sebastián overview

Peine de los Vientos

Monte Igueldo

Plaza de Funicular

Funicular

Paseo del Peine de los Vientos

Isla de Santa Clara

Castillo de la Mota

Monte Urgull

Museo Naval

Paseo Nuevo

Museo San Telmo

Iglesia San Vicente

Basílica de Sta. María del Coro

Mercado de la Bretxa

Aquarium

Puerto El Muelle

PARTE VIEJA

Teatro Victoria Eugenia

Alameda del Boulevard

Hotel María Cristina

Ayuntamiento

Plaza Guipúzcoa

Parque Alderdi Eder

N

0 metres 300
0 yards 300

Bahía de la Concha

Avenida de la Liberta

Pl. Cervantes

CENTRO

Playa de Ondarreta

Jardines de Ondarreta
Avenida Satrustegui

Playa de la Concha

Pl. Zaragoza

Pl. Zubieta

Paseo de la Concha

Calle San Martín

Catedral del Buen Pastor

C. Pamplona-Iruña

Avenida Zumalacárregui

Paseo Miraconcha

Calle General Pa

Parque Zubimusu

C. J. Maria

Plaza Alfonso XIII

Palacio de Miramar

Avenida Zarautz

C. Palacio

Calle Easo Real

Paseo Pío Baroja

Parque Básoerdi

Estación Amara

Parque Amar

Parque Araba

Pl. Benta Berri

C. Palacio

C. Palacio

C. Portuene

Plaza Izurun

Plaza Europa

Grupo Donosti Zarra

Plaza Lazkano

Paseo Izostegi

C. Pedro M. Collado

Parque Miguel Unamuno

Parque Ibaeta

Avenida Tolosa

Plaza Ibaeta

Camino de Vista Pinos

Calle Iza

Plaza Sta. Cruz

Plaza Alkiza

Parque Otxanda

Plaza Guarnizo

Paseo Bordari

Parque Melodi

Paseo Berabera

Palacio de Aiete

Paseo Aiete

Calle Katalina Eleizegi

Plaza Zapatari

Paseo Lizariz

Plaza del Deporte

Plaza de los Árbutos

Paseo de los Árbutos

Jardines Ayete

Paseo Mandi Alai

Camino del Alto de Errondo

Plaza América

Calle Xavier Lizardi

Paseo Olite

Calle Otxoki

Paseo Berabera

Paseo Oriamendi

C. Mertzegal

Plaza Aduna

Avenida Tolosa

Parque Orio

## Map symbols

🚌 Bus station
🏥 Hospital
✉ Post office
🛒 Market
⛪ Cathedral, church
🏛 Museum
ℹ Tourist information
◁ Related map
1 Detail map

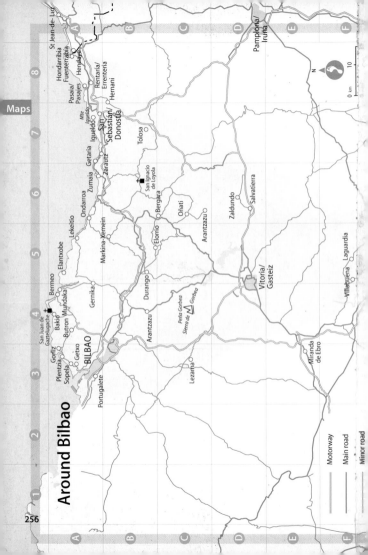

Maps

256

# Around Bilbao

St Jean-de-Luz
Hondarribia
Pasaia/ Fuenterrabía
Pasajes    Hendaye
Rentería/
Errenteria
Hernani
Pasaia/
Pasajes
Mte
Igueldo
Igueldo
San
Sebastián/
Donostia
Getaria
Zarautz
Tolosa
Zumaia
Ondarroa
San Ignacio
de Loyola
Lekeitio
Bergara
Oñati
Elantxobe
Markina-Xemein
Elorrio
Arantzazu
Zaldundo
Salvatierra
Bermeo
Mundaka
Gernika
Durango
Vitoria/
Gasteiz
Laguardia
San Juan de
Gaztelugache
Bakio
Butron
Gorliz
Plentzia
Sopela
Getxo
BILBAO
Arantzazu
Peña Gorbea
Sierra de Gorbea
Villabuena
Portugalete
Lezama
Miranda
de Ebro

N

0 km    10

A  B  C  D  E  F
1  2  3  4  5  6  7  8

Motorway
Main road
Minor road